Twayne's United States Authors Series

Sylvia E. Bowman, *Editor*

INDIANA UNIVERSITY

John Hersey

JOHN HERSEY

By DAVID SANDERS

Harvey Mudd College

(TUSAS) 112

Twayne Publishers, Inc.   ::   New York

Library of Congress Catalog Card Number: 67-13177

Grateful acknowledgment is made to Alfred A. Knopf, Inc., for permission to quote from Mr. Hersey's work, and to the *New Yorker* magazine, original publisher of *Hiroshima*.

A Bell for Adano—Copyright 1944 by John Hersey
The Child Buyer—Copyright © 1960 by John Hersey
Hiroshima—Copyright 1946 by John Hersey
The Marmot Drive—Copyright 1953 by John Hersey
A Single Pebble—Copyright © 1956 by John Hersey
The Wall—Copyright 1950 by John Hersey
The War Lover—Copyright © 1959 by John Hersey

MANUFACTURED IN THE UNITED STATES OF AMERICA BY
UNITED PRINTING SERVICES, INC.
NEW HAVEN, CONN.

FOR
MARY-FRANCES

Preface

THIS BOOK is an introduction to the work of a writer who has described himself as a "novelist of contemporary history." Hersey is one of many such novelists, but his approach is distinctive. He has not written the kind of novel in which the protagonist defines the conditions of the time in the process of discovering himself. He has not written fiction as the record of his own effort at such a definition. Nor has he been driven merely to work up material on a succession of topical issues. He differs from Saul Bellow and from Norman Mailer, on the one hand, and, on the other, from several dozen writers such as Allen Drury, James Michener, and Irving Wallace. What kind of writer Hersey is, aside from these contrasts, is the subject of this first book about him.

Hersey first confronted "contemporary history" as a correspondent for *Life* and *Time* during World War II, and the first chapter of this study considers the special advantages and limitations of this opportunity. This experience led to the epithet of "inspired journalism" being applied indiscriminately to all of his work, whether reviewers admire *Hiroshima* or decide that no true novelist would write such books as *The Wall* and *The Child Buyer*. It has also led Hersey to become active on behalf of causes and to uphold convictions that most of his colleagues—novelists or reporters—have shunned. This book is about a stretcher-bearer, a school-board member, a speechwriter for Adlai Stevenson, and a college master at Yale University—all in the line of duty as writer.

As this study moves from his reporter's background into separate analyses of the novels, it seeks to characterize a writer who cannot be restricted by narrow definitions of a literary genre or by stereotyped notions of a writer's behavior. The nature of Hersey's career precludes tracing any careful pattern of development or any recognizable scheme of a life work. Therefore, the organization of this book may seem fragmentary since its only sequence is the order in which Hersey's books have been published. There is nothing like Yoknapatawpha County or the sudden eruption of *In Our Time* in this man's work, nor anything so reassuring for a critic as the measurable development of the craft of Wright Morris. On a smaller scale, Hersey's career to early 1966 resembles the protean venture of John Dos Passos from *One Man's Initiation* to *Mr. Wilson's War.*

Long passages from Hersey's works are sprinkled through these chapters because it would be inaccurate and misleading to suggest otherwise the variety of content and form that appears in his eleven books. These passages and the reluctance to say anything final about this author are reminders that Hersey may write as many more books as the eleven summarized here, that they may be fully as significant as any of these, and that they will almost certainly be far different from anything he has already published. Granted, one may claim this prospect for any reasonably healthy writer, but it is especially significant in the case of a "novelist of contemporary history" who is open to possibility as few other novelists permit themselves to become. In fact, the only limitation which this stance has imposed upon Hersey comes in the recurrence of the theme of survival in everything that he has written, for his writing is full of the special urgency with which contemporary history has invested this subject. The present study may suggest why he specifies survival instead of annihilation, or even absurdity, and if such insistence has led him to oversimplify what he has observed and imagined.

This work is unaccountably the first book to have been written about John Hersey; moreover, it may be added to an incredibly brief checklist of everything that has been written about him. Therefore, I wish that it might have done him the small service of estimating just how important a writer he will seem fifty or a hundred years hence, or to state simply if he is now a greater or lesser writer than J. D. Salinger, John Updike, or James Jones. I am fairly certain that he would have been more esteemed by critics in the 1930's or in Upton Sinclair's heyday when American writers thrived on a contemporary history less bewildering than the recent record of atomic destruction and genocide. I believe that Hersey is one of the significant talents among many first-rate American writers and that his career has a special interest which sets him apart.

I am grateful to many people and institutions for help and kindness given me while I wrote this book. The Committee on Research and Publication of Harvey Mudd College granted me funds for study and manuscript preparation. The Honnold Li-

Preface

brary, Claremont, and David Davies were especially cooperative.
John J. Espey gave me valuable information about a missionary
childhood in China. Murray Berman, of the Pomona (California)
Public Library permitted me to study his Hersey check-list, and
Professor Ted Weissbuch called my attention to Hersey's story,
"A Fable South of Cancer."

I am particularly indebted to Mrs. Glenn Thompson for an exceptionally careful typing of the manuscript. Professor Sylvia E.
Bowman, the editor of the Twayne series, made several important
suggestions after a meticulous reading of the original manuscript.
My colleagues Ray Browne and George Wickes gave me welcome
encouragement; and, as always, my work was made possible by
my family in Claremont, Los Angeles, and La Jolla. Finally, I
must thank John Hersey for an afternoon at his home in Connecticut, for his patience since then in answering questions, and for
the loan of materials I could not have obtained otherwise.

Grateful acknowledgement is made to Alfred A. Knopf, Inc.,
for permission to quote from Mr. Hersey's work and to the *New
Yorker* magazine, original publisher of *Hiroshima*.

DAVID SANDERS

Harvey Mudd College
Claremont, California

Contents

Chronology

1914   John Richard Hersey born June 17 in Tientsin, China; son of Roscoe and Grace Baird Hersey.

1920- Attended the British Grammar School and the American
1924   School, Tientsin.

1924   Returned to the United States; attended Briarcliff Manor (New York) public schools.

1927- Attended Hotchkiss School, Lakeville, Connecticut.
1932

1932- Attended Yale University, where he was a football letter-
1936   man and a reporter on the *News*.

1936- Graduate study in eighteenth-century English literature,
1937   Clare College, Cambridge, on a Mellon Fellowship.

1937   Worked as Sinclair Lewis's secretary in the summer; joined the staff of *Time* in the fall.

1939   Assigned to *Time's* Chungking bureau.

1940   Married Frances Ann Cannon, April 27.

1942   *Men on Bataan* published in July. Assigned to the Pacific Theater for *Life* and *Time*. On October 8-9 accompanied United States Marine Corps units in the third battle of the Matanikau River, Guadalcanal.

1943   *Into the Valley*, July. Assigned to the Mediterranean Theater, where he covered the invasion of Sicily.

1944   *A Bell for Adano*, February.

1944- Assigned to Moscow. Visited ruins of Warsaw and Tallinn,
1945   where he saw evidence of German atrocities.

1945   Pulitzer Prize in fiction awarded to Hersey for *A Bell for Adano*, May 8.

1945- Assigned to China and Japan for *Life* and *The New*
1946   *Yorker*.

1946   "Hiroshima" appeared in *The New Yorker* on August 31; published as book in October. Text read in its entirety over national radio network.

1946- One of the founders and editors of *'47—The Magazine*
1948 *of the Year.*

1948   Beginning of memberships in the Authors League of America and in other writers' organizations, often as an officer and always as an active member.

1950   *The Wall,* April.

1950- Awards typical of the recognition Hersey received for
1951 *The Wall:* Doctor of Hebrew Letters, Dropsie College; citation for "improvement of inter-group understanding" from Philadelphia Fellowship Commission; citations from the Freedom Foundation of Valley Forge and from the Sidney Hillman Foundation.

1952   Active campaigning for Adlai Stevenson for President.

1953   *The Marmot Drive,* November. December 12: at thirty-nine, Hersey was the youngest writer ever elected to the American Academy of Arts and Letters.

1954   March 21. Member of the National Citizens Commission for the Public Schools, first of many activities on national and local levels of public education.

1956   *A Single Pebble,* June. Worked as a speech-writer for Adlai Stevenson.

1956- Visited relocation camps near the Austro-Hungarian
1957 border; wrote the continuity for a United Nations film on the situation of Hungarian refugees.

1957   June 10. Doctor of Literature, Wesleyan University.

1958   June 4. Married Mrs. Barbara Day Addams Kaufmann.

1959   *The War Lover,* September.

1960   *The Child Buyer,* September.

1963   *Here to Stay: Studies in Human Tenacity,* January.

1965   *White Lotus,* January.

John Hersey

CHAPTER *1*

'The Liveliest Enterprise of Its Type'

I From a Missionary Household

JOHN HERSEY was born in 1914 of American missionary parents in Tientsin, China, where he spent the first ten years of his life. A child in an American household in a foreign country, he was isolated from that country and aware of the United States only through the conversations of his parents and his older friends and by what he could read in books and magazines.

Such a childhood has severe disadvantages for someone who later becomes a writer. He lacks the sense of place of people who have a native region and grow up in it. The place that he has to remember is, instead, the missionary compound or the walled-off residential quarters of a mining camp—an insulated colony of Americans and near-American foreigners, native servants, and native workmen who go back to their homeland at night. Such a child may read and even write more than do other children because he has little else to do. As a child, he writes fantasies of a peculiar kind, which are not especially fantastic to him since they are as close to life outside the compound as he can imagine it.

Shortly after he learned how to read and write, he amused himself with the now lost "Hersey News" which carried reports on the family's activities along with whatever might be made of the daily routine in the Tientsin Grammar School and The American School, institutions serving the compound and such other children, very few of them Chinese, who knew enough English to keep up with the work. Summer vacations were spent at the seashore riding donkeys, but Hersey remembers almost nothing about a trip around the world he made with his mother when he was three years old. When he eventually volunteered information about this childhood, he remembered it as having been "no more exciting than the average child's."[1]

It may not have been, for Hersey has never written about it directly. His later articles on China carry a few slight references to these early years, but they certainly betray a sympathy for their subject that may have come in part from his Tientsin childhood. Memories play some part in the diligent construction of Chinese backgrounds in *A Single Pebble* and *White Lotus,* but a smaller part than research does. Some understanding of the effect such a childhood may have upon a future war correspondent and novelist may be gained by reading *Minor Heresies, Tales Out of School,* and *The Other City* by John Espey, whose parents were Presbyterian missionaries in Shanghai. Espey is almost exactly Hersey's contemporary, and his books, coincidentally enough, were published by Knopf after many of their chapters had appeared as sketches in the *New Yorker.* Pearl Buck is, of course, the best-known American writer born in China; but her childhood, recorded in the early sections of *My Several Worlds,* was spent somewhat earlier in an inland city under vastly different conditions from those found in Tientsin or in Shanghai.

Hersey was in the United States throughout his adolescence and young manhood, and he experienced life at Hotchkiss, Yale, and Cambridge, a summer as Sinclair Lewis's secretary,[2] and some apprenticeship at the editorial offices of *Time* magazine before returning to China as a war correspondent in 1939. There, in the wartime capital on the upper Yangtze, he found a refugee China little like the country he had known as a child, and he had no chance to study it closely. Always on the run, he noted battles, bombings, and civilian hardships; met Generalissimo Chiang and General Chennault; and flew to Japan to interview Foreign Minister Matsuoka and United States Ambassador Grew. Hersey began his overseas duties for *Time* at the pace which would make him one of the most widely and quickly traveled reporters of World War II, and this first stop in China was one of the quickest. Three days on Guadalcanal would come to mean much more to him, as would three weeks in Sicily. None of his war experiences would affect him more deeply than the Soviet-guided tour of the sites of German atrocities in Poland and the Baltic States. His return to China after the war was, however, more important. There, despite the nation's unsettled state in the winter of 1946, he was able to pick up threads which would guide him from his mission childhood through war correspondence to becoming a novelist.

In reports published by *Life* and the *New Yorker*, Hersey recorded impressions of Peiping and Shanghai, Ichang and "Red Pepper Village," the "Communization of Crow Village," and transporting of units of the Nationalist New Sixth Army by LST's from Shanghai to the north.[3] All are revealing in some degree, but the last report shows more of the transformation from outsider to novelist. Hersey was aboard an LST commanded by an American officer who strongly resembled the captain in *Mr. Roberts*. The man had simple, emphatic views on China, American politics, and the United Nations; his personal life had been even simpler: "The only two things he seemed ever to have enjoyed were nailing shingles on roofs, which he had once done professionally, and the time he had temporarily deafened his wife during a squirrel shoot by firing his gun too close to her right ear."

This skipper was extremely apprehensive about transporting dirty "Chinks" on his ship after several recent trips with comparatively clean "Japs." Disgusted with this man's petty tyrannies and the matching rudeness of most of his junior officers, Hersey spent more time than he had planned talking to the Chinese. He found out that several of them were from Tientsin, and he used this discovery to open a conversation with a Major Chow. "I like people from Tientsin," Hersey reported himself as having said. "What's good about them?" his new acquaintance replied. "They seem to me happier and straighter than people from Shanghai," said Hersey. Major Chow then surprised him by tossing this comment at the earnest, sympathetic correspondent: "They're lazy. They have no patience. They fight a lot. A man can only lie once to them, and they will fight. But, on the whole, the people of the North—the people of Hopeh, Shantung, Shensi, Shansi, Kansu—all know how to suffer." The comment was untranslatable to the captain, and it was barely understood by Hersey himself.

All the while, another American aboard had stood somewhat apart from the rest; this man, a "Lt. Jackson," had been assigned by the army as liaison officer with the Chinese units and had hung around during Hersey's conversations with Major Chow while working out for himself the irony of his own helplessness on a mission for which he was entirely unprepared because of his total ignorance of the land, the people, and the language. However, Lt. Jackson uttered something that would lead more deeply into Hersey's rediscovery of China than Colonel Chow's remarks or the memories dredged up from Hersey's childhood. "They laugh easier than any people I ever saw," said Jackson about the troops who were huddled miserably on the LST's deck. "I used to wonder why these Chinese were so backward. I reckon I'm beginning to know—they're just so happy the way they are, they don't want to change." Yet a moment later, he asked Hersey, "Did anyone ever call you a *yang kwei tze* (a white devil)?"

In this conversation one may find, at the very least, the basic themes of *A Single Pebble*, Hersey's first Chinese fiction, which would be described admiringly upon its publication as a "novel of revelation." Awareness of all the strange ways in which one might be a *yang kwei tze* were to stir twenty years more in Hersey's creative imagination before they appeared in *White Lotus*.

Although the incident suggests a source for one of his novels and measures long-delayed effects of Hersey's Tientsin childhood, it points as well to Hersey's strengths and problems as a writer. With a keen eye for the conditions of men's lives, he has held the utmost sympathy for his fellow human beings. This sympathy has often produced sudden, simply-stated generalizations about the human condition. It has also made Hersey's writing more overtly purposive than the works of most of his contemporaries; it has also made Hersey a less subjective writer than almost any other novelist now at work.

His experience, even if so much of it has been on the run, has shown him that many of the people he has met and observed have led far more tragic or heroic lives than his. Their lives as survivors of Hiroshima or the Warsaw ghetto, as marine infantrymen or Peiping ricksha boys, have been more illustrative of the fundamental conditions of this century. But he has not written guiltily as a spectator compensating for his failure to participate; instead, he has had an uncomplicated idea of what he must do. The same sense of responsibility—awakened by his sympathy—that led him to become a stretcher-bearer on Guadalcanal, or to chair a committee on school conditions in Fairfield County, or to speak to Major Chow also underlies everything he has written.

But, as the incident on the LST reveals, Hersey is no simple writer-evangelist. He has learned as he has written, however rushed learning and writing may have been on occasion. If his conscience has been persistent in Hersey's career, so also has been an unappeasable curiosity with all of its consequences for a man's development. Conscience and curiosity, indeed, invested Hersey even at the time toward the end of the war when he might have seemed so easily secure with a recent Pulitzer Prize, still everyone's "imperative reading," and a popular candidate to write the definitive fiction of World War II. He was in a remarkably easy position to become a celebrity—or, worse, to practice the self-obsession which has distracted so many of his colleagues. However, the author of the breezy *A Bell for Adano,* product of a few intense weeks during the invasion of Sicily, became a vastly different writer by the time of *The Wall,* five years later, after a much more intense experience—seeing German concentration camps in Estonia and then the ruins of Warsaw— *and* years of reflection and meticulous reporting and scholarship.

But to speak now of the author of *The Wall* or *A Single Pebble* is to get too far ahead in an account of John Hersey, just as to proceed directly from the Tientsin household through all of his schooling to World War II would be to put off tediously the beginning of the story. Hersey must be seen first as the war correspondent for *Time* and *Life* who earned bylines early in his career, had his picture published beside those bylines (suntans, helmet with captured netting, large eyes set in a lean face), published the "imperative books" and finally won the Pulitzer Prize on V-E Day.

II *Journey to the Matanikau*

Hersey had decided very early to become a reporter, perhaps as early as when he wrote the family news sheet. By the time he found himself on a Mellon Scholarship at Clare College, Cambridge, studying eighteenth-century English literature, he had narrowed his ambition to working for *Time.* "I was aware that I might have to wait a long while until there was an opening, but I didn't care," he said. *Time* seemed to him "the liveliest enterprise of its type," and he wanted, "more than anything, to be connected with it."[4] While he spent some months in the summer of 1937 as one of a succession of secretaries to Sinclair Lewis, the opening at *Time* materialized far more quickly than he had expected. The Japanese invasion of North China had begun that same summer, and a staff opening developed sooner than any normal course of rotating assignments. His evident knowledge of the area, even more his *feeling* for the material coming in from China, could not escape the notice of his superiors on a magazine whose chief had himself been born in Tientsin, the son of American missionaries. Hersey was off in 1939 to the Chungking bureau, headed by Theodore White; from there he flew all over the Chinese front and Japan, writing a few dispatches of the action and interviewing military and political leaders.

In whatever may be conjectured as Hersey's work in the generally anonymous *Time* war columns of those years, one notices more the training of a reporter than the development of any particular ideas or the expression of any of his characteristic sympathies. Hersey was taxed with keeping up with the "liveliest enterprise of its type" more than he could have been concerned with anything else. Pacifism, flourishing in the undergraduate and Cambridge University atmospheres from which he had so recently emerged, had to be set aside—just as the table talk of a missionary household held little lingering gaiety for a young man indignant over the Japanese campaign in China. Hersey is for that matter, somewhat exceptional among American writers in the 1940's for having been aroused first by the Japanese actions rather than by those of the Nazis.

Yet, even antipathy toward the Japanese was stifled on such an assignment as his interview of Joseph Grew in Tokyo.[5] With faintest sarcasm, Hersey observed that, in the summer of 1940, "Japanese-American friendship (had) suddenly become a pressing matter." The McCormick and Patterson newspapers were arguing for the practical necessity of a strong Japan, along with numerous experts who merely advanced the old maxim that it was better not to court trouble on two fronts. Ambassador Grew, Hersey noted, was trying to prove a lifelong belief that "a gentleman can always get the better of a tough guy by continuing to act like a gentleman." A Grotonian and a Harvard man like President Roosevelt, Grew frankly advocated befriending Japan; and, according to Hersey's interview, he was enormously successful: "After his complaints about the *Panay*,[6] 70,000,000 Japanese considered themselves personally responsible to him." Hersey called Grew's program "dynamic appeasement," a strange phrase to set beside the persistently hostile references to "Japs" in the reporter's later stories.

The Grew interview was Hersey's only by-line before Pearl Harbor. His Far Eastern assignment was transient enough to permit several flying trips back to the United States, on one of which in April 27, 1940, he married Frances Ann Cannon, the daughter of Martin Luther Cannon, the cotton goods manufacturer of Charlotte, North Carolina.

Hersey emerged from the anonymity of *Time's* masthead in June, 1942, with the publication of his first book, *Men on Bataan*—one that is peculiarly the work of a *Time* staffer habituated to the practice of reducing piles of notes and cabled material to truncated columns headed CHINA or WAR IN THE PACIFIC. *Men on Bataan* was written in New York with *Time-Life* files at hand, as well as with some original material from friends of General MacArthur, families of other servicemen, and interviews with Carl Mydans and Melville Jacoby, *Time* writers who had been at the action. Produced just a month after the surrender of Corregidor, *Men on Bataan* was the only kind of book that could then be written about the desperately bad news of the Philippines fighting since most firsthand observers were either imprisoned in the islands or fighting from new posts in Australia and the South Pacific. Of course, twenty years later one may question why the book needed writing at all and why someone who hadn't been there took it upon himself to write it. Cynical answers must be dismissed as one examines the tone of the writing for suggestions of Hersey's motives. "You ought to know them for they are like you," Hersey wrote in his first chapter about the men on Bataan. "They have reacted as you will react when your crisis comes, splendidly and worthily, with no more mistakes than necessary." The writer, plainly caught up in the war effort, was doing a book that he felt had to be published for the sake of morale and truth in this year of American defeat.

Men of Bataan consists of alternate chapters on General Mac-Arthur and the men who fought under him in the Philippines. The MacArthur chapters make up a small-scale biography beginning with the general's boyhood at army posts; the chapters on his subordinates cover the four months' fighting following December 7. The quickly contrived structure shows Hersey working much more successfully with the men than with the general, with actual operations than with the less tangible question of command. MacArthur was, frankly, a forbidding figure for the writer. First in his class at West Point, first army officer to become a field marshal (a Philippine appointment), first member of the Rainbow division, first or foremost in virtually everything with which his name could be linked, he was too heroic to be packed into a quickly written, neatly edited war book. Quoting the man made things worse: "By God, it was destiny that sent me here." Hersey tried to be level-headed about MacArthur; he noted that it was important not to react too skeptically to the MacArthur myths.

Fifty vignettes dealt with the approximately fifty thousand other men who fought on Bataan. Often, such an account would be about a group of specialists under a particular leader, as in the case of Captain Aaron Abston and his anti-aircraft gunners. Commander William Bulkeley, of the PT boat flotillas, was represented as one of the individual heroes gaining wide notice. Captain Colin Kelly, then believed to have sunk the battleship *Haruna* by crash-diving into its main stack, was celebrated along with the Filipino flyer, Jesus Villomar. Hersey noted Father Duffy, counterpart and namesake of the World War I chaplain in MacArthur's Rainbow Division. He took pains as well to write of individual enlisted men such as Sergeant Joe Stanley Smith, one of the unlucky New Mexico National Guardsmen stationed on Luzon in 1941. "His sensations by his own account later took in everything from hot flashes to the calm a man feels only on the toilet seat," Hersey wrote of Sergeant Smith, an observation which might serve as a transition between the broad secondhand montage of many heroes in *Men on Bataan* and the altogether different book Hersey would write next when he had accompanied a patrol himself on Guadalcanal.

Men on Bataan was extravagantly praised, but *Time* gave it perhaps the least sweeping tribute. Fletcher Pratt, in a special issue of *Saturday Review of Literature* devoted to morale and edited by Eleanor Roosevelt, said that *Men* was "literature that will not be read with shame after the war," as so many novels and personal histories of World War I were presumably being read with shame in 1942. (*Three Soldiers* and *A Farewell to Arms* were being condemned on this very ground in Archibald Mac-Leish's contemporary polemic, *The Irresponsibles*.) In an utterly faithful reaction to the moment, Mr. Pratt judged that the book "should be read by every participant in the struggle." S. T. Williamson, in the *New York Times Book Review*, pronounced it "cloth-bound journalism at its best." The *Time* reviewer saw the book as especially fit for a "hero-hungry United States."

Even as these reviews were being written, Hersey was in the South Pacific at the Battle of the Solomons, at which point it is extremely important to credit him with certain profound changes as a journalist, although it must be acknowledged that some narrowness or perhaps merely a distance from his subjects persisted. The great change was that he began to see the war firsthand, separating himself forever from the class of person who would either write or read *Men on Bataan.* Also for the first time, at least since childhood, he had immediate, active objects for his compassion. Throughout college and in the early years with the Luce publications, Hersey was a severely frustrated humanitarian. He had to contend with *Time*style in life as well as in print: that assurance that "the liveliest enterprise of its type" could effectively understate the world's woes and hit near the truth. In the Solomons, he was freed from any compulsion to write about distant heroes. Although his accounts often continued to include asides addressed to build the morale of the nation, he took commendable advantage of the opportunity to report combat action. He also risked his life beyond the requirements of his assignment.[7] A significant turning point in his career came with his participation in the third battle of the Matanikau River, Guadalcanal, October 9, 1942.

Hersey's baptism of fire occurred during a typical Guadalcanal action with a comparatively small number of marines engaged in one of several attempts to force the Japanese away from the sluggish stream which was the natural defense line for Henderson Field, five miles to the east. The first battle of the Matanikau had been a frontal assault which failed because the attacking forces were too small; the second was an encircling maneuver which had failed for the same reason. The third effort entailed a decoy holding attack at one point, another at the actual crossing point, and a third force behind these on the flank. After being briefed by colonels Simms and Merrit Edson (organizer of the first marine raiders), Hersey was attached to Company H of Simms' regiment, under the command of Captain Charles Rigaud.

Although Hersey learned as much about the forthcoming action as any intelligent layman might with the help of a map and the colonel's briefing, it should be stressed that the correspondent had no idea of what would happen to him in the next two days. "If I had had any understanding of what Company H might meet, I never would have gone along," he wrote candidly in the *Life* article[8] and in the eventual book, *Into the Valley*. Actually being under fire was only one of the facts of this mission of which he was ignorant; the company *was* pinned down by snipers and mortars at one point as it proceeded in single file to the river. Later the marines were encircled, and the correspondent was suddenly in a position to know fear when a fabricated order for withdrawal began to be passed back man to man through the line until it was calmly and abruptly stopped by Captain Rigaud. On the way out, Hersey saw a dead marine whose "bitter young face said, as plainly as if he had shouted it, 'the Japs are bastards.'" Finding a Japanese corpse shortly afterward, he stripped its helmet of the netting and placed it over his own, wondering who the owner might have been. It was a rare instant of wondering for Hersey in his Pacific Theater service, where Japanese were never considered men with personal histories. Only Americans were individuals in the Pacific war; "the jungle was Jap."

Hersey could never have anticipated the physical hardships of the march: the heat, the chafing skin and aching muscle, the weight of a pack on his back, the whole contest between mountainous jungle terrain and the human body. The greatest revelation came with the care of the wounded, where he was able to note the comparative comfort of a man with a severe shoulder wound besides the total indisposition of "Bauer" with a mortal abdominal wound. He saw a combat surgeon operating in the half-light of the jungle, administering plasma to an officer near death, and so enabling the man to walk back to a jeep in which he would ride sitting up back to Henderson Field. Hersey helped carry the stretcher bearing "Bauer," who stirred to consciousness only long enough to ask for help so that he could defecate and, having done this, died.

Hersey's accounts of Bauer's agony and Rigaud's quiet efficiency stand out along with his own muted personal experience from the rest of *Into the Valley*. The book was an effort, he declared, to recapture the feelings of those on the mission because "the battle, and especially the skirmish with Rigaud, illustrated how war feels to men, everywhere." He added fervently: "If people in their homes could feel those feelings for an hour or even just know about them, I think we would be an inch or two closer to winning the war and trying like hell to make the peace permanent." He reported well enough in *Into the Valley* to do without such statements; but the earnestness, however baldly expressed, is characteristic of Hersey's writings and sounds better now than some of the loftier morale pronouncements in his later articles for *Life*. It was typical of Hersey to plead, however cursorily, for the permanent peace as well as for his readers' compassion toward fighting marines. He makes the point more effectively in the middle of the book when he states that the men fought, above all, "to get the goddam thing over and get home." In the welter of notations on "Jap bastards" and "Jap jungles," there are reassuring indications of the beginnings of the sensitivity which would develop in *The Wall* and *The War Lover*. Hersey wrote much else in 1942 and 1943 that rings less true.

The account of the battle on the Matanikau, for example, was preceded on November 9 by a "think-piece," "Marines on Guadalcanal," complete with some of the illustrations by Major Donald Dickson, USMC, and later to be published with *Into the Valley*. The first sentence read: "Marines are human." Those that followed nurtured public stereotypes:

> As a fighter, he is a cross between Geronimo, Buck Rogers, Sergeant York, and a clumsy, heartsick boy. . . . He has barren amusements and longs for letters. . . . He kills because in the jungle he must, or be killed. . . . He has an understanding of the war that it will take most Americans a long time to get. . . . He is not well informed of the outside world. He is resentful of the government, Navy, Army, and General MacArthur. . . . He sings a song that goes, "the Army has the medals, the Navy takes the queens, but the boys what takes a rooking are the United States Marines."

So defined are the men Hersey accompanied to the Matanikau. The reader gratefully remembers "Bauer" and Captain Rigaud.

The highlight of the 1943 Christmas number of *Life* was a thirty-two page portfolio of paintings by its artists-correspondents (Aaron Bohrod, Fletcher Martin, and others) titled "Experience in Battle." The text, written by John Hersey, contains the perfunctory solemnity required by the occasion and the format, but there are several passages in which Hersey continued to define the feelings he had reported so vividly in *Into the Valley*. Again he mentioned hatred of the Japanese enemy: "call it neurosis, call it hatred that consumes men and never leaves them, call it whatever you wish, the feeling of men who have fought the Japanese is permanent and terrible." Such hatred, however, may not have been what drove American soldiers to kill, Hersey was willing to acknowledge. He was puzzled for many years over the seeming paradox of men who killed and yet loved life above anything else. Kill or be killed failed to explain it: "For American soldiers, who know their duty when they see it, but who love life so very much, the Japanese warrior code is beginning to be a thing of pity. It says 'Duty is weightier than a mountain, while death is lighter than a feather.' The marines who fought on Guadalcanal wanted only to live to fight victoriously another day and, after the fight, to be happy and relaxed and American for many other days."[9]

This statement falls short of *The War Lover* in explaining the fighting man's primal urge to survive; but it does begin to reveal why, even in the midst of accounts Hersey devoted to action, the theme of survival persisted. American fliers were neither cruel nor insensitive, he wrote in the column beside Floyd Davis's paintings of the Hamburg raids; the war would end sooner for them, and their scars would heal quicker if they could concentrate coolly on hitting the enemy carefully and well. (Except for Chungking, Hersey had seen little of the results of aerial bombardment.) The Purple Heart, he wrote to accompany Aaron Bohrod's paintings of the wounded in the Pacific, "is not only the common symbol of all experience by battle, but is also a badge of hope that some day men may live together without the urge to kill."

Hersey was on Guadalcanal little more than a month. He had been with the aircraft carrier *Hornet* for an even shorter time before that. These assignments and others were punctuated by brief returns to New York, so that he had less time at a given battlefront than was allotted the average correspondent; he had less time in the Solomons, for example, than Richard Tregaskis.[10] Hersey had little more time with any one outfit than he had with Company H as it went into the Matanikau Valley, so that he did not immediately gain as intimate an understanding of the war as did many writers who would produce novels or personal histories based on their commitments to a single campaign or military unit.

He had, on the other hand, a truly spectacular view of World War II, perhaps the broadest view afforded any American writer. From the Solomons he was sent to Sicily and subsequently to Russia. He was able to interview men from all the fighting services and from many of the special areas within each service. He met an equally varied assortment of the war's civilian victims. He was among the first to write about the returning veteran. He reported occupation, liberation, and rehabilitation. The nature of his assignments permitted him to speculate on the peace earlier than almost anyone else. He had also unwelcome, oracular functions that most correspondents were privileged to avoid. In a sense, until well past V-J Day, he was never entirely free of the compulsions that led him to write *Men on Bataan*: the need to attempt the impossible explanation of war aims when no one could be entirely lucid about why he was fighting. He was assigned to ask questions of Russian novelists, American military governors, and PT boat captains that could only have brought the most guarded, cryptic, or vague answers. Hersey's dispatches, reread long after the war, enable one to discover how much information there was about the war while it was being fought and, at the same time, how much cloudy commentary there was about its significance. How meticulously American publications reported the most obscure phases of a military operation! How vaguely men wrote about war!

Hersey rose to the top of his profession between 1939 and 1945. A sensitive young man with a special yet limited background, he saw instances of life and death fleetingly and vividly; had moments of a reporter's access to the subtleties of military command and political power; saw—if very quickly—perspectives of war on land, at sea, and in the air. And he saw work, suffering, pleasures, loneliness, madness, despair, heroism, and routine. Hersey was also luckier than many of his colleagues. *Time* writer Melville Jacoby was killed in a jeep accident in Australia after getting safely off Bataan. *Time* writer Jack Belden was wounded in Italy just a few months after he had survived an overland hike following an airplane crash between Chungking and Calcutta.

Hersey had quite a bit of luck with his stories, too. He filed the first account of Lieutenant John F. Kennedy's experiences after the destruction of his PT boat.[11] He followed up an interesting day's visit with the American military governor of Licata, Italy, by writing *A Bell for Adano*. He interviewed the survivors of Hiroshima, having overcome whatever hatred of the Japanese he had felt while writing of Guadalcanal.

Because World War II was fought more globally than any earlier war, because air transport had become commonplace, and because news coverage had become more varied, detailed, and instantaneous than ever before in history, John Hersey, among many American war correspondents, had an opportunity given no earlier writer. Because of this very opportunity, he faced altogether new handicaps. As he was about to become an imaginative writer, he stood somewhere between the wire service editor in the Middle West who created a novel of the Russian front, *Retreat from Rostov,* from his ticker tape and the combat infantryman (Harry Brown or Norman Mailer, for example) determined to write coherent fiction about his experience.

And this situation should lie at the heart of any discussion about Hersey as novelist—not the narrow, sufficiently answered question of whether a reporter may write novels. Rather, can any man see so much so quickly and broadly and proceed to make any sense of it? As Hersey himself asked later, how is the novelist to address himself to contemporary history? This task is certainly not the same as turning news into fiction, as any comparison between *A Bell for Adano* and *The Wall* will prove. Contemporary history, as Hersey came to understand it, was something that could be based on as unchangeable a circumstance as the command routine of "Red Pepper Village" in North China or on as complete a revolution in man's prospects as the nuclear bomb. The foregoing review of his war correspondence shows that he was concerned with the relation between news and contemporary history. A writer who would seek to define the relationship on the spot at any time between 1939 and 1945 would stumble over the imperatives of wartime morale and the editor's deadline on significant statements. Hersey had not gone very far into the question when he turned one of his wartime news stories into his first novel.

III   A Bell for Adano

Shortly after covering an unusually violent engagement early in the Sicilian campaign, Hersey dropped by the office of the American military governor of Licata, a seaport on the southern coast of the island which had been part of military history since the Punic Wars. What he saw very obviously impressed him and was recorded in a *Life* article, "AMGOT at Work" (August 23, 1943). With a few pictures, it covered two of the back pages in *Life*.

The dispatch was an unpretentious description of a day's work for the military governor. The unnamed, dark-skinned, mustached major was described as "energetic in a La Guardia kind of way," which is vaguely inaccurate.[12] The major who sits at a desk dispensing justice, making notes, and tossing off orders between interviews is more reminiscent of Sancho Panza governing his "island" than of La Guardia running New York. During the day, two women are denied permission to travel to Palermo because there is no available transport. A well-dressed merchant is told why his draft notes on the Bank of Sicily are temporarily worthless. Another merchant is told to prepare a fair price list for food and clothing that had been impounded by the Fascists. An eighty-two-year-old man warns the major about the black market. A cartman is brought to trial for impeding traffic, and his case is dismissed. A wealthy householder is awarded damages for casual vandalism by American troops. A pretty girl is told that her sweetheart is alive as a prisoner of war. Almost everyone gives an absent-minded Fascist salute. The parade of visitors does not end until Hersey and the major leave abruptly for lunch. After they return, the parade will continue because every citizen of Licata has access to the military governor's office.

Working three weeks in the month of September, 1943, Hersey expanded this article into *A Bell for Adano*. Each person mentioned in the article became a character in the novel, each problem that came before the actual major's desk was stretched into an incident, and each broad comment about American military government became a principal theme. Beyond this, Hersey added a character who resembled General Patton, and he created the central situation of the village bell. Knopf published the novel on February 7, 1944, and the reviews ranged from the

enthusiasm of Orville Prescott in the New York *Times*[13] to Diana
Trilling's cold comment in the *Nation* that the book smacked of
contrived simplicity, that the author's "ideas, like his prose,
have undergone a process of conscious, falsifying, and purposeful simplification.[14] Except for *Hiroshima, A Bell for Adano* has
been Hersey's most widely read book.

Today, *A Bell for Adano* seems not to have deserved the
praise given it in 1944 when reviewers were apparently overwhelmed by the prospect of affirmative war fiction. Mrs.
Trilling, on the other hand, surely made a narrow, if not
malicious, inference about the writer. Hersey wrote a simple
book in a hurry, which is not at all the same thing as "falsifying simplification." His story with all of its implications—all of
the ideas Mrs. Trilling found "falsifying simplified"—is at hand
in the first paragraph of the *Life* article.

> For a long time we have taken pleasure in the difficulties met
> by Germany and Japan in organizing the conquered lands. Here
> at the major's desk you see difficulties, hundreds of them, but you
> see shrewd action, American idealism, and generosity bordering
> on sentimentality, the innate sympathy of common blood that so
> many Americans have to offer over here. You see incredible
> Italian poverty, you see the habits of Fascism, you see a little
> duplicity and a lot of simplicity and many things which are comic
> and tragic at one time. Above all you see a thing succeeding and
> it looks like the future.

Review and excerpt may also point to the great gap existing in
1944 between a correspondent's perspective on war happenings
and the reflections of a literary critic in Morningside Heights
on the war's significance.

On the other hand, Mrs. Trilling may never have recovered
from the foreword to the novel. It states that Major Victor
Joppolo is a good man and that the reader should know him;
furthermore, the United States, with the invasion of Sicily, is in
Europe to stay, and its efforts there will depend more on the
Joppolos than on the Atlantic Charter or any current theories of
how Europe should be liberated and rehabilitated. This statement represents the Hersey who wrote glosses for *Life's* war
paintings or noted that nothing means more to a serviceman
than mail from home. The hero and his problems are more
effectively introduced in the first few pages of the story when he

steps ashore as the port is being secured and makes his first decision. The Via of October 28, named for the date of Mussolini's march on Rome, will henceforth be known as the Via of July 10, date of the landing. Fascism ends for Adano. Whatever system replaces it remains to be defined in the future. Joppolo, meanwhile, gets to work.

He is almost exactly as Hersey had described the subject of his *Life* article: dark-skinned, mustached, of Italian parents, a New Yorker who had worked at several small jobs before entering the army. He feels the "sympathy of common blood" very keenly: "it's a hell of a note when we do that to our friends," he remarks upon seeing his first Italian corpse. He touches his palm to the dock immediately upon arrival and is upbraided by his cynical sergeant for being "sentimental." Hersey might have intended to make more of the sergeant in the course of the novel, since he is identified as Joppolo's "assistant conscience" and is given a far more colorful set of credentials than his superior. (He is a refugee Hungarian journalist who has lived in Marseilles, Rome, Boston, and San Francisco before unaccountably finding himself an enlisted man in the United States Army.) However, most of his sarcasm is spent by the end of the first chapter, and he contributes nothing to many incidents of Adano's occupation where someone's hard-boiled commentary would have been welcome.

Joppolo takes over the old office of the *podesta* of Adano, a great hall in the *palazzo di citta*. On the way in, he has noticed the empty clock tower whose bell had been taken away and replaced by a whitewashed Fascist slogan: "The Italian people built the Empire with their blood, will make it fruitful with their work and will defend it against anyone with their arms." This statement provokes a speech that is typical of Joppolo, the idealist: "If they have seen any fruit of their work, they would have fought with their arms. I bet we could teach them to want to defend what they have. I want to do so much here . . ." (7). Here, and in the pages following when Borth jokingly compares the major to Mussolini, the novel is off to a shaky start with pronouncements that democracy is replacing Fascism.

Attention to the bell itself comes none too soon with the first Italian to present himself to the occupation authorities: Zito, the old doorman, was an anti-Fascist; but he had to eat, earn a living, and support six children. He summarizes the town's

condition very effectively. The people have been without bread
for three days; the old authorities have escaped; the dead are
unburied; the water carts haven't gotten to town for several
days; no one believes in victory any more; and the bell is gone.
He elaborates only upon the bell. Everyone had lived by the
bell. It was seven hundred years old, had rung in every hour of
their lives, was the one thing that linked them to an awareness
of what they were as human beings. "When the bell spoke, our
fathers and their fathers far back spoke to us," says the eighty-
two-year-old sulphur merchant, Matteo Cacopardo. "It told us
when to have the morning egg and when to have pasta and
rabbit and when to drink wine in the evening," says the fat
Craxi. "I think it was the tone which mattered," says Zito. "It
soothed all the people of this town. It chided those who were
angry, it cheered the unhappy ones, it even laughed with those
who were drunk. It was the tone for everybody." "All life re-
volved around it," says Father Pensovecchio. American Military
Government instructions haven't prepared Joppolo for such an
emergency, and he must fall back on the most important of
"Joppolo's notes to Joppolo": "When plans fall down, improvise."
He thereupon promises to get another bell—and makes the most
important decision of his career in military government.

One story line is thereby set in motion, and it is highly entertaining. The second has to do with General Marvin. At about
the time that Joppolo was setting up his office in Adano, General
Marvin's progress along Sicilian roads was suddenly halted by a
sleeping cartman whose mule and vehicle were standing in the
middle of the road. The general waves his riding crop, then
shouts, "goddam you goddam cart get off the road." The cartman continues asleep; the general orders wagon, mule, and
driver thrown off the road into a ditch. When the mule screams,
the general orders it shot; at this point the cartman finally awakens
to begin sobbing with the dead animal in his arms. General
Marvin's party then proceeds into Adano to check with town
authorities on the outrage; and Major Joppolo is left with an
order prohibiting all carts from entering Adano. General Marvin
storms out of town; but, when Joppolo learns that the town's
water supply depends on those carts, he countermands the order.
The second story line, therefore, consists of the news of Joppolo's
insubordination catching up with General Marvin. A succession
of enlisted men from all over the Mediterranean theater keeps the

official papers bouncing around in courier's bags and lying at the bottom of the pile on appropriate desks for almost as long as it takes Joppolo to replace the town bell.

Hersey, who had been somewhat reticent in writing about General MacArthur in *Men on Bataan,* was altogether direct in creating a character whom all of his readers would recognize as having been based on General George S. Patton:

> I don't know how much you know about General Marvin. Probably you just know what has been in the Sunday supplements.
>
> Probably you think of him as one of the heroes of the invasion: the genial, pipe-smoking, history-quoting, snappy-looking, map-carrying, adjective-defying, divisional commander; the man who still wears spurs even though he rides everywhere in an armored car; the man who fires twelve rounds from his captured Luger pistol every morning before breakfast; the man who can name you the hero and date of every invasion of Italy from the beginning of time; the father of his division and the beloved deliverer of Italian soil.
>
> You couldn't be blamed for having this picture. You can't get the truth except from the boys who have come home and finally limp out of the hospitals and even then the truth is bent by their anger.
>
> But I can tell you perfectly calmly that General Marvin showed himself during the invasion to be a bad man, something worse than what our troops were trying to throw out. (47-48)

When Hersey wrote the novel, Patton's slapping of two shell-shock cases was common knowledge among correspondents and thousands of servicemen in the North African and European theaters. By the time the book was published, the incident had been released to newspapers and had become a national scandal. A smaller story at that time mentioned that Patton had ordered a mule cart thrown off a bridge and then ordered the mule shot. A few months afterward, Patton had become publicly "rehabilitated" because of the singular success of his tank units in breaking through the Normandy perimeter across France to the Rhine.

Hersey made no public comment on Marvin as Patton. No one felt the need to ask him. It is a one-sided characterization which ignores any of Patton's warrior virtues, perhaps because the story has nothing to do with military operations. Beyond being Joppolo's antagonist, Marvin is an enemy of the peace, a narrow war lover.

With his story lines set early, Hersey skillfully developed the notes taken at the major's desk in Licata into several entertaining episodes. His quick eye and his quick sympathies worked well. There is the fiery Cacopardo, whose great moment comes in facing General Marvin at the moment that the mule-killer is playing mumbletypeg on an antique table, and informing him that he is a barbarian. Overcome by his rage, Cacopardo forgets to tell the general what he knows about the disposition of German forces. The fierce hatred of authority shown by the fisherman, Tomasino, is well portrayed. Hersey easily might have made the man a routine anti-Fascist, but he caught instead the genuine anarchism of the Mediterranean working man that had been noted by few other American writers besides Dos Passos.[15] Tomasino's daughter, who attracts Joppolo, is commendably ordinary. Her sister is described as more voluptuous, and the girl has dyed herself a blonde out of sheer restlessness with Adano. The town crier, Mercurio Salvatore, blusters just enough to escape becoming a complete buffoon. The village priest, despite the contrived name of Pensovecchio, is not the usual clerical stereotype of liberated Europe rushing out to greet his Christian deliverers. He only addresses Joppolo once as "my son."

The incidents involving these people all bear out some large or small decision by Major Joppolo; and each decision proves the opening thesis that he is "a good man." The effect of *A Bell for Adano* is, therefore, very much like that a reader may gain from the episodic display of the marine biologist's goodness in John Steinbeck's *Cannery Row*—except for Hersey's preoccupation with his political theme.

A Bell for Adano was pre-eminent among the American fiction of World War II for a very short time, and its reputation depends upon whether it is held surpassed by Harry Brown's *A Walk in the Sun* later in 1944 or by Thomas Heggen's *Mr. Roberts* in early 1946. It was sensational for its portrait of Patton, but it was didactic from the first page in warning readers of the pitfalls toward peace. The "generosity, bordering on sentimentality" ascribed to Major Joppolo often describes Hersey's own attitudes this early in his career toward his subjects. However, he wrote plainly, entertainingly, and feelingly—not quite so well as in the best parts of the patrol action on the Matanikau, but better than in almost any other part of his war correspondence.

IV V-E Day and After

Hersey was awarded the Pulitzer Prize in fiction for *A Bell for Adano* on May 8, 1945. In the New York *Times,* beneath oversized headlines proclaiming the end of the war in Europe, a small front-page box announced this award. Almost every other newspaper in the world blazoned the day's event in larger type and accordingly pushed the Pulitzer story to the inside pages. It was a fitting moment for the first phase of John Hersey's career to reach its climax. His first novel, besides winning the prize, had been turned into a Broadway play and subsequently into a motion picture; it was also serialized and condensed in the American press, and even translated for Soviet publication. Hersey's assignments for the Luce publications began to vary significantly, and his frequent visits to New York were crowded with speaking engagements and award presentations.

At that moment, he was burdened by the same extravagant praise and belittling slurs that had been heaped upon other celebrities, actors and athletes and all of the "ninety day wonders" in and out of uniform, who had come into notice since Pearl Harbor. He could not agree with Orville Prescott that he exemplified a new breed of war writer, who, unlike the men who wrote about World War I, could "look beyond both horrors and heroics and tell the truth to the best of their ability."[16] Nor, as a man who had published his first novel eight years after throwing an undergraduate effort into the incinerator, could he be assured by statements that he had written a "magnificent parable" or that he had "everything needed to make a front-rank novelist" because of his "consuming interest in men and women and a genuine love for them."

There are ironic parallels to his own situation in a report Hersey cabled from Moscow, which appeared in the book section of *Time* (October 9, 1944). Hersey or the section editor borrowed Gorki's phrase to entitle the piece, "Engineers of the Soul." "Not a word is written which is not a weapon," Hersey said of Soviet wartime writing. (He was not innocent of the old slogan, "art is a weapon," raised decades before the German invasion. He was aware that he himself had been "disarmed," in a sense, by Soviet authorities, who had confined him to Moscow with other Western correspondents and allowed him to learn of the Red Army's westward progress only by the salvos fired in Red Square for each liberated city.) The books that he chose to summarize for his report could not be criticized in conventional terms: "The only fair test is to see whether writers have fulfilled their aims." And in Russian wartime writing, writers were explicit about their aims. Hersey saw it very simply: they hated the enemy, and all their energies were committed to defeating him. They had taken part in the war: "Much more than our polemicists on the Writers' War Board, much more than our warriors of the Office of War Information, more even than most of our war correspondents (certainly than those in Moscow), the Russian writers have been in and out of the war."

In his own way—not that of Sholokhov or Simonov or Vizhnevsky—Hersey had been in and out of the war. Professionally a spectator, he had been a participant privately. The pattern of his working operation had been to go from panorama to close-up; he was as mechanical in his outlook as he had been in his dispatches. The war had been made up of individuals to be reported quickly and vividly: name, rank, home town; conspicuous feature or expression; characteristic action; a minute's candor; and something in the man's own words. Sometimes the names were changed to avoid embarrassing their families. The war had been fought by all of the major powers of the world, over most of the planet's surface; it had been a shifting struggle between black and white areas on a map; and it had been a war less characterized by slogans ("to make the world safe for democracy," "*drang nach osten*") than by such bludgeoning abstractions as "fascism," "democracy," "liberation," and "unconditional surrender." They too had to be reported and could scarcely be omitted from the smallest dispatch.

Hersey grew most as a writer during this experience when he considered how men survived their ordeals, as he did in the account of Lieutenant Kennedy for the *New Yorker*, in the moments when Captain Rigaud stopped panic in the ranks, or in inspecting the sites of German atrocities. Otherwise, Hersey at the end of the war was the man who had had to write too much too soon.

CHAPTER 2

Hiroshima

HERSEY'S greatest war reporting came after V-J Day with *Hiroshima*, which may be treated as a book or as an event. A short, factual account of the lives of six Hiroshima residents after the bomb was dropped, it is so objective and so understated that the *Times Literary Supplement* reviewer observed that is "spoke too quietly." More than any of the previous news stories or photographs, this book most enlightened the American reading public about history's least imaginable event.

I Assignment in China and Japan, 1946

In September, 1945, Hersey was commissioned by the *New Yorker* to do a series of articles on the effects of the atomic bombings. Since *Life* had also re-assigned Hersey to the Far East, it was arranged by the two magazines to share the correspondent's expenses for a period of several months in China and Japan in late 1945 and early 1946. Several articles on postwar China followed in short order: sketches of ricksha men, missionaries, American marines, and North China villagers. Some of them dealt with the precarious balance of power between the Chinese Communists and Nationalists; others simply concentrated on personalities. A few of them indicated no change of pace from the casual interviews he had been writing all along. Others, such as "Red Pepper Village," "Two Weeks' Water Away," and "The Happy, Happy Beggar," show an obviously subtler understanding of human beings than may be found in *A Bell for Adano* or in most of the earlier pieces for which the writer had been praised for his love of men and women.

Life in "Red Pepper Village" was the sharpest available contrast with a reporter's wartime settings.[1] Try as he might to make sense of village life within the context of what he understood the contemporary struggle to be, Hersey was forced to a recognition of its timeless routine. He was faced with a country that he had had little chance to understand as a child in Tientsin: "the China which goes on forever . . . inhabits hundreds of thousands of places like Red Pepper Village, which absorbs its conquerors and plants its crops and pays no mind to political fashion." Here were people whose "horizon of understanding coincide[d] with the visual horizon"—a perspective then diametrically opposed to Hersey's own. Painstakingly, he was seeing more within his "visual horizons" and thereby making his "horizon of understanding" less a grab-bag of historical stereotypes. Visiting Red Pepper Village contributed to Hersey's altered vision in *Hiroshima;* in it there are no Major Joppolos tagged as "good men" and no side references to the United Nations Charter as a guide for avoiding such holocausts in the future.

His "Letters" to the *New Yorker* during the several months preceding his arrival in Hiroshima concentrate on Chinese places. "The Happy, Happy Beggar" is the story of Father Walter P. Morse, of the Episcopal order of the Cowley Fathers, a missionary in Ichang in the dead center of China near the mouth of the great Yangtze Gorges, the farthest point of Japanese penetration during the war. A detailed, sympathetic portrait of "the happiest adult" Hersey had ever known, this "letter" marked the first time this child of missionaries had ever written about an American religious worker.

Generally and politically, Hersey's comments on the unclear months after the liberation are more critical of Chiang and the Nationalists than they are of the Chinese Communists, but it would be an exaggeration to say that he wrote sympathetically of the Communists. He felt that they *should* be called Communists instead of "agrarian reformers." He mentioned that they *had* contributed their bit by the spring of 1946 to the destruction of the agreements so painstakingly negotiated by General Marshall. Actually, his only political sympathy in China was evoked by the hopeless cause of the Democratic League, whose leaders were "for the most part, mild, gentle, rather frightened-looking, but really quite courageous professors, lawyers, doctors, and other professional people."[2] Such leaders got eggs thrown at them in 1946. Hersey concluded that, no matter what the United States did, China was in for "a long, sharp, bloody struggle." Years later, in *Witness,* Whittaker Chambers named

Hersey as one of a clique of *Time-Life* staff members who had slanted content to favor the Communists.[3] The accusation was neither pursued nor denied. The evidence of what Hersey did publish on China as a Luce employee (not to mention any cursory examination of *Time* and *Life* China copy, generally, between 1946 and 1949) suggests that Chambers severely distorted the facts.

The last stop on his trip was Hiroshima, which Hersey reached in the late spring of 1946. He was at liberty to report what he saw in any way he might choose,[4] and he had several options. Life in the city months after the bomb was itself a terrifying enough picture of destruction to be his subject. From many interviews he might have developed a single panorama of the target at impact. He might have restricted himself to vivifying the statistics, making concrete the abstract descriptions of a nuclear explosion, objectifying generally this single common knowledge of so many thousand victims and so many square miles of ruins—all that most Americans had grasped of the occurrence. He did, indeed, travel through all of the damaged area; interview many more persons than eventually appeared in the book; and, for his own understanding, turn cold statistics into tangible evidence.

But, as he organized his early notes, he decided to concentrate on six persons who were chosen only because they had been good interview subjects, and not for any more dramatic reasons such as their closeness to ground zero or the extent of their sufferings or because they made up any convenient cross-section of Hiroshima. He had the *New Yorker's* traditional, three-installment serialization in mind; and he planned to refocus on the original scene—"the noiseless flash"—at the beginning of each installment. When he returned to New York with his manuscript, *New Yorker* editor William Shawn made the decision to publish all of it at once in the issue of August 31, 1946, which devoted its entire editorial space to the finished story. Ten sixteen-hour days of rewriting, with Shawn and Harold Ross[5] standing by, produced the present four-part article which takes six people from the hours just before the "noiseless flash" to the time when the author met them the following spring. The distinctive tone of understatement was unchanged from the first drafts.

II Hiroshima: *A Story of Six Survivors*

No generalization can be made about Hersey's six people except that they survived the bomb. They were two doctors, a German priest, a Japanese Methodist minister, a housewife, and an office girl. No deliberate contrasts were set up between any two of them. Father Kleinsorge and Reverend Tanimoto are variously solicitous, stupefied, heroic, and disheartened. Each does one thing after another in no particular pattern determined by their personalities or their backgrounds. Similarly, young Doctor Sasaki happened to have been the only staff member of the Red Cross Hospital to have escaped injury and therefore worked for three days without stopping. Dr. Fujii had his small private clinic blasted out from under him. He "had hardly time to think that he was dying before he realized he was alive," but he survived in a pitiful state of fractures and lacerations to stumble out of town to refuge. Mrs. Nakamura, although hurled through her house as the bomb struck, survived uninjured along with her three children; but Miss Sasaki crushed under a pile of books in her office, lay untended for days with a compound leg fracture.

What Hersey does take pains to trace is the individuality of these random survivors. One of them values a particular possession; another had a special plan that the bomb shattered; another was marked by some extraordinary vanity. Neither ennobled nor made grotesque by the details stressed, each person has his own story that complements the sweeping catastrophe.

The book begins at the moment the bomb was dropped, in a passage which states where each of the six was and what he was doing. It is quoted in most sustained references to *Hiroshima* somewhat misleadingly as the example of all that follows. The rest of the paragraph, as a matter of fact, says far more of Hersey's intentions: "A hundred thousand people were killed by the atomic bomb, and these six were among the survivors. They still wonder why they lived when so many others died. Each of them counts many small items of chance or volition—a step taken in time, a decision to go indoors, catching one streetcar instead of the next—that spared him. And now each knows that in the act of survival he lived a dozen lives and saw more death than he ever thought he would see. At the time, none of them know anything" (4). *Survivors. Why they lived. Act of survival.*

These words are basic to *Hiroshima,* even more basic than death and suffering. The book is a memorial to the dead and a warning to the living, but it is, above all, an examination of those who survived by a writer clearly more interested in the acts of survival than in anything else he saw at the scene of a hundred thousand deaths.

When the bomb fell, the six potential survivors were in various states of anxiety and exhaustion. Hiroshima and Kyoto, alone among major Japanese cities, had been spared the B-29 raids; and such people as Reverend Tanimoto wondered if something special were being saved for the city. Father Kleinsorge had been sick with diarrhea, Mrs. Nakamura had been up most of the night before at an air raid shelter bedding down her three children, Dr. Sasaki had felt feverish and sluggish and had a nightmare, and Miss Sasaki worried about her fiancée who hadn't written her for a long time. Reverend Tanimoto was considered a "security risk" by some of his acquaintances because, in addition to being a Christian, he held a degree from Emory University and spoke English well. Father Kleinsorge was a conspicuous white foreigner.

When the bomb fell, each of them was turned away from the flash:

Mr. Tanimoto has a distinct recollection that it travelled from east to west, from the city toward the hills. It seemed a sheet of sun. . . . He felt a sudden pressure, and then splinters and pieces of board and fragments of tile fell on him. He heard no roar. . . . (8-9)

As Mrs. Nakamura stood watching her neighbor, everything flashed whiter than any white she had ever seen. She did not notice what happened to the man next door; the reflex of a mother set her in motion toward her children. She had taken a single step (she was 1,350 yards, or three-quarters of a mile, from the center of the explosion) when something picked her up and she seemed to fly into the next room over the raised sleeping platform, pursued by parts of her house. (12-13)

He [Dr. Fujii] saw the flash. To him—faced away from the center and looking at his paper—it seemed a brilliant yellow. Startled, he began to rise to his feet. In that moment (he was 1,550 yards from the center), the hospital leaned behind his rising and, with a terrible ripping noise, toppled into the river. The doctor, still in the act of getting to his feet, was thrown forward and around and over; he was buffeted and gripped; he lost track of everything, because things were so speeded up; he felt the water. (15)

After the terrible flash—which, Father Kleinsorge later realized, reminded him of something he had read as a boy about a large meteor colliding with the earth—he had time (since he was 1,400 yards from the center) for one thought: A bomb has fallen directly on us. Then, for a few seconds or minutes, he went out of his mind. (18)

He [Dr. Sasaki] was one step beyond an open window when the light of the bomb was reflected, like a gigantic photographic flash, in the corridor. He ducked down on one knee and said to himself, as only a Japanese would, "Sasaki, *gambre!* Be brave!" (20)

Just as she [Miss Sasaki] turned her head away from the windows, the room was filled with a blinding light. She was paralyzed by fear, fixed still in her chair for a long moment (the plant was 1,600 yards from the center). Everything fell and Miss Sasaki lost consciousness. The ceiling dropped suddenly and the wooden floor above collapsed in splinters and the people up there came down and the roof above them gave way; but principally and first of all the bookcases right of her swooped forward and the contents threw her down with her left leg horribly twisted and breaking underneath her. There, in the tin factory, in the first moment of the atomic age, a human being was crushed by books. (22-23)

With only this last detail that even approaches distortion, the short introductory section is closed. The twenty pages are compact, tightly but not quite contrivedly organized, with many of the hardest maxims of expository writing carefully obeyed. The account is clear, vivid, crisply coherent, and utterly unmarred by any lingering impulse that Hersey may have had to say more about the first atomic bomb than the details themselves conveyed.

The second section of *Hiroshima* (much the most informative to readers who wanted to know about the atomic destruction) is about the next few hours as the great fire swept over the city. The six survivors react in such ways as to prove the writer's assertion that at the time they knew nothing. Reverend Tanimoto, who emerges as the only person making his way *into* the city, described himself as running in fear away from the suburban house, where he had gone on an errand, toward the center of the city where he thought he might find his wife. It was, indeed, incredibly fortunate that he did find her running toward him as he got closer to town, but such is the tone of the report that the reunion is barely noted as "incredibly fortunate" before the reader is pulled away toward other scattered lives and Reverend Tanimoto himself is propelled into confused acts of mercy.

Dr. Sasaki "worked without method" at the hospital as streams of the walking injured began to fill the dressing station and hospital courtyard. Tanimoto and Sasaki were luckier at the moment than Father Kleinsorge, whom the bomb had left in a stupor, vaguely aware of his own cuts and bruises as he became increasingly appalled by the greater injuries he saw about him. As people, buried beneath the fallen timbers of their houses, screamed to be rescued from the onrushing flames, the priest was committed to saving a Mr. Fukai, the Catholic mission secretary, a man who sobbed that he wanted to be left behind to die. After a while, Father Kleinsorge had to leave—in his dazed state, someone else seemed more in need of rescue—and Fukai ran back to his own immolation.

This incident serves as well as any of several others to illustrate the quality of understatement in *Hiroshima*: the reporter's determination to let facts speak for themselves. All that Fukai is quoted as saying is "leave me here to die." Not even through Father Kleinsorge's immediate reaction to the man's request nor in any coloration of Fukai's words does Hersey permit any comment on this phenomenon of despair. His desire to die runs directly counter to the instinct for survival, the major theme of Hersey's report; but the reader is not told within the chapter that Fukai may have sensed something final and hopeless about this bomb that set it apart from the fire bombs that were desolating almost every other Japanese city. There is no underscoring the fact that this cry is uttered by a Japanese Catholic, nor does Hersey state directly that Fukai was, indeed, the only person in the whole account who fled from the possibility of survival. A few pages later in the third section it is explained in passing that once, just before the raid, Fukai had told a priest that Japan was dying and that, when it came Hiroshima's turn to be bombed, he wanted to die with his country. With the reader engrossed at that point in the struggles and schemes of the survivors, it seems even more appalling that, of all the persons who must have uttered such sentiments as Fukai's in the obviously final days of the Empire, he should be the only one to act upon them. In the summer of 1946, as the popular imagination increasingly described the advent of a nuclear age as either the beginning or the end, it is astonishing that this doomsday advocate was so completely underplayed.

Meanwhile, Miss Sasaki was removed from beneath the pile of books only to be summarily dumped under a lean-to to wait days for medical attention. Mrs. Nakamura moved still with a mother's instinct toward safe ground with her children; and Dr. Fujii, wounded worse than he knew, arose painfully from the wreckage of his hospital in the Kyo River to wonder if "a Molotov flower basket could have done all this."

The wind blowing over Hiroshima brought large rain drops while it advanced the great fire. To this point, it might be observed, Hersey had written nothing about the technical properties of the bomb. Most of his readers were aware that something called "radiation sickness" existed, and a few may have had a rough timetable in mind of what might occur at zero plus one or two or three. Hersey's account, however, is strictly limited to the "visual horizon" of his six survivors; and it so skillfully renders the details of that horizon as to establish suspense for even his best informed readers.

While the third section continues the parade of suffering and traces the pattern of reaction to disaster, it pushes ahead toward such explanations of the bombing as would come to the victims in the first few days. "Details Are Being Investigated" is an ironic tag for the helpless efforts made by Japanese authorities to appease the victims' terrified curiosity. As survivors huddled together in Asano Park, a naval launch moved up and down the seven rivers of Hiroshima and a young officer on deck shouted through a megaphone that a hospital ship was on the way to take care of the situation. By this time it was early evening of August 6, the day the bomb was dropped; about half of *Hiroshima* covers this time period. In the pages of this third section, the reader is taken up to August 15, which he will have difficulty in remembering as V-J Day.

Some of the details appall the curious. Father Kleinsorge stumbled upon a group of soldiers whose eyes had melted in their sockets (the single most horrifying detail in the book), but they were alive and thirsty. The priest made a drinking straw of a thick grass blade so that they might draw water through the swollen apertures which had been their mouths.

"Since that day," Hersey wrote, "Father Kleinsorge has

[46]

thought back to how queasy he had once been at the sight of pain, how someone else's cut finger used to make him turn faint. Yet there in the park he was so benumbed that immediately after leaving this horrible sight he stopped on a path by one of the pools and discussed with a lightly wounded man whether it would be safe to eat the fat, two-foot carp that floated dead on the surface on the water. They decided, after some consideration, that it would be unwise."

Having gotten a rowboat, Mr. Tanimoto meanwhile began ferrying wounded from the fire to Asano Park, and, at that point, from the water to the shore, only to discover that some of the victims, unable to move from where they had been left at the edge of the water, drowned as the tide rose. Having found his wife and left her in safety, he finally made his way back to his parsonage and discovered in one scene some evidence of the odds against him in his role of shepherding people toward life— the life of a continued existence after the wreckage, not for the moment the life everlasting which he had been preaching. The young Mrs. Kamai, whose husband had just been conscripted days before and was probably among the dead, was bent over the ground clutching her dead infant daughter. She held the corpse for four days: "Once he tried to suggest that perhaps it was time to cremate the baby, but Mrs. Kamai only held it tighter. He began to keep away from her, but whenever he looked at her, she was staring at him and her eyes asked the same question. He tried to escape her glance by keeping his back turned to her as much as possible" (76-77).

After nineteen hours spent dressing wounds, Dr. Sasaki crawled away to sleep only to be awakened within an hour and dragged back to care for the victims who continued to stray silently into the hospital courtyard. On this second shift he was told that someone had discovered exposed X-ray plates in the hospital cellar.

Mrs. Nakamura and her family were among fifty refugees taken into the chapel of the Jesuit novitiate. After two days and nights under propped-up roofing in the yard of the tin factory, Miss Sasaki was evacuated from Hiroshima. Dr. Fujii drank Suntory whiskey in a friend's summer house outside town, applying cold compresses to his broken collarbone and mulling over the rumor that the bomb had really been a kind of fine magnesium powder sprayed over the city, which exploded when it came in contact with the high tension wires of the city power system. A concurrent, less comprehensible, rumor had it "that the city had been destroyed by the energy released when atoms were somehow split in two. The weapon was referred to in this this word-of-mouth report as *genshi bakudan*—the root characters of which can be translated as "original child bomb" (82).

The concluding section of *Hiroshima*, "Panic Grass and Fever-few," hurries from August 15 to the time when Hersey actually interviewed the six atom bomb survivors. Those who had not been discernibly injured when the bomb was dropped began coming down with variations of radiation sickness. On the twelfth day, Father Kleinsorge was suddenly exhausted and his apparently negligible cuts had opened wider and become swollen and inflamed. Mrs. Nakamura's hair began falling out as she combed it. Reverend Tanimoto felt tired in the middle of a heavy workday restoring his parsonage, lay down, and fell asleep. He spent one month lying down in a friend's house, his fever once reaching 104 degrees; then he spent another month recovering on the island of Shikoku. As all of these people began to re-cover from radiation sickness, it became apparent to them that they lacked some of the energy they had had before, a fact which was especially noticeable in the most energetic of the six, Reverend Tanimoto. It was as though the simple tiredness that all of them, for various reasons, had felt on the night of August 5 had come back to them as a general malaise. It had returned to contend with their decision to live as nearly full lives as they could possibly put together again.

All six survivors re-established themselves in the city, for by November, 1945, the population of Hiroshima had returned to 137,000, one-third of its wartime peak. This figure is carefully balanced beside the number of the dead, which moved from the officially accepted 78,150 to the certainty that at least one hundred thousand had perished and that the exact number could never be reached.

"The lives of these six people, who were among the luckiest in Hiroshima, would never be the same," Hersey stated, in con-cluding his report. And how did they feel about the bomb a year later? Reverend Tanimoto was mostly impressed with how people had borne up under it. Miss Sasaki prepared for con-version to Catholicism (under Father Kleinsorge's instruction), although she was unable to come out of deep depressions when she thought of how she would be a cripple for the rest of her life. Dr. Sasaki thought that those who had decided to use the bomb should be brought to trial along with the certified war criminals in Tokyo. Dr. Fujii and Mrs. Nakamura felt that there was nothing to be done about it: *das ist nichts zu machen, shikata ga nai.* The reader may infer Father Kleinsorge's opinion as Hersey quotes the report of another Jesuit in Japan: "The crux of the matter is whether total war in its present form is justifiable, even when it serves a just purpose. Does it not have material and spiritual evil as its consequences which far exceed whatever good might result? When will our moralists give us a clear answer to this question?" (117).

III   *Hiroshima as an Event*

The reception of *Hiroshima* was unusual by any standards.[6] A New York *Times* editorial printed the day after the *New Yorker* was circulated called urgent attention to the article: "every American who has come to regard them [the bombs] as one more sensational phenomenon ought to read Mr. Hersey." Albert Einstein was reported to have ordered a thousand copies and Bernard Baruch five hundred. Requests by newspapers for serialization rights were granted on the condition that the profits be donated to the Red Cross and the article be run unabridged. The Book-of-the-Month Club distributed free copies to all its membership. Harry Scherman, its director, said, "we find it hard to conceive of anything being written that could be of more importance at this moment to the human race." Within two weeks of its publication, the article was read on four hour-long radio programs on the American Broadcasting Company at "prime time" competing with Fred Waring and "Mr. District Attorney" at nine o'clock.

The distribution of *Hiroshima* was virtually world-wide by the end of 1946, with one ironic exception. The American Occupation Authority in Japan, which had been unable to police the pamphlets of Japanese nuclear physicists, prevented the distribution of *Hiroshima* with stubborn effectiveness.[7] Under questioning of the Authors' League, in April, 1948, General MacArthur's headquarters insisted that the book had not been banned; but when the League cabled back asking if this message could be taken as authorization of the Japanese publication of *Hiroshima,* it received no answer. In June, Japanese publishers made their largest post-war acquisition of American titles, but neither *Hiroshima* nor *A Bell for Adano* was listed among the ninety-one sanctioned books. Hersey's plans for Japanese publication had stipulated that his profits should go toward rebuilding Reverend's Tanimoto's church. Reverend Tanimoto, despite his loss of energy, had asked to do the translation.

Hiroshima has been an enduring work throughout twenty years in which the potential of thermonuclear destruction has dwarfed the explosion of August 6, 1945. Perhaps this book endures because, fortunately, no one can write anything like *Hiroshima* about the hydrogen bomb. What this weapon might accomplish has been repeatedly and lucidly hypothesized in thousands of articles, but none of these warnings has had the full admonitory effect of Hersey's account. Instead, all of them have had to build upon the reader's awareness of what went on in the two victimized Japanese cities. Concrete understanding begins and ends with the details of Hiroshima, however one may state that the hydrogen bomb effect is so many times greater. The creative imagination has attempted to cope with this dilemma many times. One such result was Nevil Shute's *On The Beach,*[8] which offered a flat premise—this is the end of the world—and then proceeded to develop a web of human relationships that were quite easy to follow. In the 1960's came Stanley Kubrick's motion picture, *Dr. Strangelove,* and the end of the world became a comic motif. The theme of survival was mocked hilariously when the film ended with noiseless mushroom clouds filling the screen as a mellow little vocal group sang:

> We'll meet again,
> Don't know where,
> Don't know when,
> But I know we'll meet again some sunny day. . . .

Hiroshima is good to reread after one has seen *Dr. Strangelove.* Hersey simply carries the theme of survival to the limits of human possibility—short of melancholy speculation or satiric fantasy. His six citizens of Hiroshima may have been among the last persons to face the limit of man's destructive capacities that will ever be unleashed; if this should prove true, Hersey will have done all that a writer could have done to make it so. Under such circumstances, it is a very difficult thing to comment on "the mind and art of John Hersey," and it is almost impossible to consider *Hiroshima* as the fourth of the writer's eleven books.

In 1963 *Hiroshima* was reprinted, along with several of Hersey's longer magazine articles, in a volume entitled *Here to Stay.* It was the last item in a collection of pieces on the theme of survival: "Studies in Human Tenacity," as the dust jacket announced. The article is reprinted unchanged and with no explanatory note except for the simple notation of the increased power of weapons since 1945. The collection was published—and one must now believe that *Hiroshima* was written as Hersey wrote it—because of the writer's conviction that "man is here to stay in spite of the appalling tools he invents to destroy himself, for it seems to me that he loves this seamy world more than he desires, as he dreads and flirts with, an end to it."

IV *Other Writings on Peace, 1946–47*

Hersey accomplished less with other ventures in the immediate post-war years. He was one of the most active of more than a hundred writers, photographers, painters, illustrators, cartoonists, and designers who tried to establish *'47—The Magazine of The Year,* which they hoped would have as great an impact as the astonishingly successful magazines which had followed World War I: the *New Yorker, Reader's Digest,* and the Luce publications themselves. *'47,* which came to resemble *Coronet* more than anything else, had little chance of surviving in a period which would see such established general magazines as *Collier's* vanish from the scene. Aside from Hersey's editorial work, his greatest contribution to the magazine was "A Fable South of Cancer,"[9] a long story about the attempt of an aircraft carrier crew to organize a workable society after their ship had run aground on an uncharted island. Their first important decision is to remain lost, a decision easy to stick to as long as the bountiful island and their own ingenuity can make them entirely comfortable after weary months of front-line action. (They are shipwrecked with far more provisions than Robinson Crusoe ever enjoyed, as well as 2,599 additional individual talents.)

Early differences among these colonists center on the ques-

tion of destroying or maintaining radio transmitters—a dispute between those who want to found a new world and those who
want to hedge. A constitution is reluctantly drawn up—an in-
comprehensible document generally approved. Government is
quite democratic with a new administrative officer every day;
distinctions between officers and enlisted men vanish as individuals prove their usefulness. A chief boatswain's mate, who
is tattooed with some of the great sayings of the Western world,
becomes an elder statesman and the lone character of any continuity throughout the tale. The society's isolation is finally broken in the spring when a substantial number of its members
find that they can't live any longer without women.

When the radio transmitters send news of the island to the
United States, the response is predictably overwhelming. The
crew of the *Thomas Jefferson* become national heroes and the
complement of future island wives becomes instantly over-
subscribed. Women do not necessarily ruin this new paradise;
rather, in 1946, the fall is precipitated by the exaggerated press
releases of a reporter who never got ashore from the ship that
brought the colonizing women. *The Islet of Peace* tells the world
about human tranquility achieved in the middle of the Pacific
Ocean. The settlers begin to believe what has been written about
them, and they promptly send their own representative to the
United Nations. This mission fails utterly when the representative provokes a riot at the first meeting he attends and is sent
back to the island by a unanimous vote of the other delegates.
Shortly after his return, a routine town meeting breaks down in
bitter disagreement over a proposal to levy taxes for building a
big town hall.

Parties form, Taxers and Anti-Taxers. An Anti-Taxer is found
murdered, and his party shortly leaves town for another part
of the island. The boatswain devises a plan to build a town hall
without levying taxes, but the Taxers reject it on the ground that
the opposition would never accept it. All communication ceases
between the factions, and reports drift of military preparations
in the Anti-Taxers' new town. War is imminent at the end of the
tale, except for the renewed spirits of Chief Burlingame. While
he is talking politics with his wife, who believes that "you can't
change human nature," one of the tattoos between his shoulder
blades begins itching fiercely, and he has his wife read it to
him: Men are not so good as their intentions; they are only as

good as their deeds. He decides to "do something," even though his wife remarks that, if he is going to do something about this island's trouble, he can do nothing more than put it off a while: "Well, if you add a while to a while . . . and then if you add a while more to that, pretty soon you have a good long time. And anyhow a while is better than no time at all. It looks to me as if we have just a little better than no time at all right now. Yes, a while will do very well . . . ."

The "fable," which reads like a condensation of the novel it might have become, plainly reveals Hersey's concern for international peace in the year and a half since V-J Day. Its message—to keep talking and put off shooting—was on everyone's lips at the time; and it formed, as anyone will remember, the bedrock justification for the work of the United Nations, once its critics had swept aside the necessity for such of its projects as *UNESCO*. Hersey also displays some of the nostalgia, now perhaps not so easily remembered, for the possibilities of the survival of an American-Russian alliance after the war against Hitler. The story is highly informative now of a state of mind as fixedly contemporary as the date of the magazine in which it appeared. The same quality, more artfully executed, had been the mark of *A Bell for Adano*. The bare "fable" was condemned, as the magazine was, to be forgotten. It had been the editors' hope to rename their magazine at the turn of every year, but they found it unnecessary to carry their plans that far.

Hersey's vigorous support of the United Nations appeared in print another time in 1947, "Alternatives to Apathy," in *U. N. World*.[10] He set forth in his militant program, "ten things that one man alone can do," thereby appealing to the denial of "putting off for a little while" with which he had concluded "A Fable South of Cancer." One man alone could do a great deal, he insisted. He should recognize at the outset that the UN was simply a start toward a world government strong enough to prevent war. Any individual interested in such a goal should join a group devoted to the study of world organization: the United World Federalists, for example.

One man alone should study and advocate such improvements in the UN as: a system of law to define and govern acts of aggression; universal disarmament supervised by the UN; a world military force more powerful than any possible combination of national forces; a provision effectively preventing secession by any UN member; provisions making the laws concerning aggression applicable to individuals as well as to nations; and criminal courts to execute the laws. A program for the UN would feature a world conference on economic problems in which the prosperous countries "would examine minimum consumption needs and productive capacities of the various people and perhaps create a world economic plan, complete with international public works and development authorities."

Hersey established himself as an authentic visionary among UN enthusiasts in 1947, and he was "farther out" than those who would merely defend the organization as a means of keeping on talking instead of shooting. These suggestions would depend, as he surely knew, upon a world of Victor Joppolos; but they were deadly earnest coming from a man with his particular memories of Hiroshima and the Eastern European death camps. The combination of earnestness and naïveté is even more pronounced in points nine and ten of his program:

> 9) Have a personal philosophy. It matters very little for the purposes of this discussion, whether the personal philosophy at which one arrives is based on the Catholic papal encyclical, *Quadrigesimo Anno*, or on the eighteenth century philosophers of democracy, Rousseau, Hobbes, Locke, or on Jefferson and the Federalists; or, for that matter, on Buddhism and filial piety; or on any other scheme. The point is that in reaching a philosophy, an intelligent world citizen is bound to realize that there are many political, economic, and religious systems in the world; he can be a more intelligent adversary of those with which he does not agree; he can also be more tolerant; he may even be able to change his opinions in a changing world. But he can do these things only if he knows exactly what he thinks at a given moment.
>
> 10) Reinforce convictions with courage. It is ironic that it should ever take courage to work for peace; but just now it does. It takes courage to fight against disinterestedness and boredom; apathy is a formidable and down-dragging adversary. Being pro-peace is nowadays equated, in many quarters, with being pro-Russian and Communistic. It is perfectly possible to disagree strongly with the Communist system and Russian methods and still work for peace; just as it was possible, during the New Deal in the United States, for a Republican to be a rabid Roosevelt hater and still be pro-democracy; or, at present, for a Democrat to be anti-Taft and still pro-American. It takes courage to act, and only by action on the part of individuals, only by going on from the basic steps out-

lined here to really coordinated political action on local, national, and international planes, can the present trend toward war be reversed. Above all, it takes courage to hurry.

Today, it is plain enough that Hersey never arrived at a personal philosophy such as those he suggested in point nine. If his beliefs can be labeled, even as loosely as he labeled possible beliefs in this article, they may be called "liberal humanitarianism." He recommended no formulated creed, but instead and always the earnest articulation of deep-set feelings of concern for the survival of the human race, even at the expense of traditions that few cautious men would surrender. Point ten, "reinforce conviction with courage," actually refers as much to his convictions as it does to his actions. "High-minded" and other adjectives one might apply loosely to a casual acquaintance fit Hersey disturbingly well. He is "high-minded," "dedicated," full of integrity in ways that resist efforts to classify his actions and character in more specific terms. These characteristics complicate criticism of his novels since any one of them can lead to oversimplified explanations that obscure Hersey's development as a novelist and the extraordinary variety of what he has written.

CHAPTER 3

The Wall:
A Novel of Contemporary History

WORLD WAR II—so called because almost everything about it had been anticipated by World War I—can be distinguished from any other war by at least two events: the atomic bombings and the extermination of six million European Jews.

Future novelists went to war in the 1940's having learned from Dos Passos' *Three Soldiers* and from Remarque's *All Quiet on the Western Front* all that they needed to know about the impersonality of modern warfare. A second world war, as far as they knew, could provide no greater break with tradition than had the first. They had read Eliot's *The Waste Land* and Graves's *Goodbye to All That*. Six years of war, as far as they could tell, actually brought nothing new despite the greater scale of aerial bombardment or the peculiarities of jungle fighting. Then came the full revelation of Hiroshima and, much more gradually, an awareness of what had transpired in Hitler's concentration camps.

The story of the camps had been hinted at throughout the war. The world had learned in the 1930's of official anti-Semitism in Germany, and there were the accounts from a few refugees. Allied forces in April and May of 1945 made the first horrifying confirmations as they overran camp sites on the roads to Berlin. Photographic evidence was brought to the Nuremberg trials. Documents, from the anonymous *The Black Book of the Polish Jewry* to Anne Frank's *Diary of a Young Girl*, began to be circulated. Yet, it remained for John Hersey, briefly an observer of the remains of atrocities in Eastern Europe,[1] to be the first American to attempt a novel about this experience. Some Americans, Jews among them, were already writing their war novels, still trying to make sense of their own involvement as a condition of understanding contemporary history.

The Wall is one of Hersey's two longest novels and is the result of his most exhausting effort as a writer. Many critics have
considered it his best book, but there is no possible way that its
virtues could be compared with those of *A Single Pebble* or
The Child Buyer. It is obviously a heroic advance over *A Bell
for Adano*—as great as if Steinbeck had gone from *The Moon is
Down* to *The Grapes of Wrath* instead of the other way. Obviously, *The Wall* has much in common with *Hiroshima* in pursuing the theme of survival—the two books share an accumula-
tion of Hersey's observations from the ruins of Warsaw to the
ruins of Hiroshima. But *The Wall* is beyond the brilliant
journalism of *Hiroshima* because of Hersey's determination to
make fiction of the history of his time. He faced his first great
creative problems in writing *The Wall*, just as he had bypassed
them five years before in filling out the details of a week in
Licata.

I *The Writing of* The Wall

Hersey is as reluctant to discuss his own work as he is willing
to praise the efforts of other writers; but, nevertheless, he has
written at some length on the composition of *The Wall*. When
he received the Howland Memorial Prize from Yale University,
his alma mater, he read a paper titled "The Mechanics of a
Novel," subsequently reprinted in the *Yale University Library
Gazette*.[2]

His first "conscious determination to write a novel on the
themes" (my italics) of *The Wall* came in 1945 when, as a
Time-Life correspondent in Moscow, he was one of several reporters taken by Soviet authorities to liberated areas of Eastern
Europe and conducted through the ruins of Warsaw, where
the ghetto had been destroyed two years before. The stark
rubble impressed him less than interviews with the survivors of
the Lodz ghetto, the sight of the funeral pyres at Tallinn, and
the warehouse-dungeon of Rodogoscz, "beside whose high walls
still lay the broken bodies of those who had preferred jumping
from upper-story windows to the horrors being transacted inside
those buildings." He was then "travelling naive in the totalitarian
jungle," but "the experience gave rise to certain optimism, too,
for in each case there were survivors, and one had to conclude
that mankind was indestructible."

The spring of 1946 in Hiroshima "lent urgency to what had

been a vague idea." Early the next year, conversations with a survivor of Auschwitz deterred him from writing about the concentration camps themselves. He had talked to a *kapo*, a prisoner who had risen by cunning and force to become a camp official, and decided that it would be better to go back to the survivors of the ghettos, who had lived as' families and communities until the end. "Because of its legendary quality," he chose the Warsaw ghetto and then began to read.

Almost at once he discovered an abundance of material, all of it in Polish and Yiddish. There were diaries, organization records, letters, statistical data, medical histories, and songs, and it seemed unlikely that much of it would ever be translated into English. (The *Black Book of the Polish Jewry* was, and he read it.) He was lucky enough to find a highly competent translator for each language; and, after several laborious experiments with other means of transcription, he had each person read directly from the original text onto a wire recorder in rapid and "intensely moving" English. (The translators are acknowledged in the "Editor's Prologue" of *The Wall* for their work on the Levinson Archive: Mendel Norbermann and Mrs. L. Danziger.)

Then Hersey lived with the tapes, which he "did not see as documentary" but "heard as felt experience." For months on end, listening to Mr. Norbermann and Mrs. Danziger, he found a mysterious change overcoming his approach to his novel. The translators, in their reading, skipped or summarized and inserted interjections; they became storytellers instead of simply translators and transcribers. They were beginning to shape his decision to tell the story through a series of first-person narratives, from the point of view of ghetto residents. He continued listening to them even as he pursued his research by reading Peretz and Sholem Aleichem and studying the Old Testament and the Orthodox prayer book. Mr. Norbermann had lost his mother in the ghetto; Mrs. Danziger, her brother-in-law. Their transcriptions made up at least half of the two million words that went into Hersey's notes and recordings before he had completed the research for *The Wall*. It was then late 1948, and he was still not ready to begin writing.

He took notes on his notes ". . . as if I were interviewing the three of us—the two translators and myself." At times in the course of his preparations he had been tempted to seek out actual Warsaw ghetto survivors; but he decided that, as a novelist, he should be no closer than the transcriptions of Mr. Norbermann and Mrs. Danziger, which were compelling enough, but still allowed him to create his own ghetto characters. Busy work occupied him for some time: a chronology of ghetto events, a list of fifty people in the ghetto whom he thought he would like to know, nineteen themes to appear in the book ("I. In danger, some men surprised into heroism; others amazed to find themselves corrupt . . . XVIII. The Wall.").

He began to invent episodes, attaching characters and themes to them. Certain characters were beginning to stick out from the list of fifty, and, among them, Noach Levinson changed from a *judenrat* official to "a kind of intuitive historian" and an ideal plotting device. In the story, yet conceived in the third person with an omniscient author, the "intuitive historian" would appear with his comments between chapters as a chorus. After a year and a half of preliminary study, Hersey had come up with an intricate plan that he believed to be final.

Writing proved disillusioning: "What I wrote down fell far short of what I had dreamed, and each day's stint was poetry unrealized, unachieved." He was unconvinced by what he had written, but stayed with the growing longhand manuscript. When he had gotten four-fifths of the way through his first draft, the metamorphosis of Noach Levinson had gone even further. His "choruses" were becoming too long to squeeze conveniently between the theme-indexed chapters, and he was aware that he would have to rewrite the whole book. Levinson—and the storytellers on the wire recorder—had won; he would henceforth be the person through whom Hersey's story would be told. It was a big and rather frightening decision for the journalist-turned-novelist to make: "This particular story needed to be told with an authority my gifts could not evoke; it needed to be told by a participant in the events; and my creature, Levinson, some of whose literary mannerisms, I confess, were annoying, did seem to me to have the gifts, the background, and above all the experience to make his story believed."

Hersey wrote much faster on the Levinson draft. As before, he charted scenes and characters and observed that the second chart "looked more like a purposeful graph . . . I could see from the bare symbols the possibility of growth, change, and rhythm in the characters." Above all, Levinson took over. He became spokesman for an author who reluctantly surrendered his own plans; then a character in his own right; and, only because of this effort at characterization (since he had run away with something in the "inner process" Hersey had not spoken about), at last an inspired mechanism for putting together a sprawling novel.

II *The Levinson Archive*

Levinson is introduced as the compiler of an archive—four million words in minute, meticulously legible Yiddish script about almost every phase of life in the Warsaw ghetto. (The million words of documents read by Hersey's translators had been written by many hands.) He is contrived as the sole source of all that could be known about the ghetto; the sole transcriber of *judenrat* business, of songs and plays; the single indefatigable recorder of his own intense observations, of everything observed or remembered by his friends that might contribute meaningfully to the record of a people. For, if Levinson is made to seem merely a recording device himself by virtue of the sheer numbers used to describe his work, it must be remembered that his work had as unifying a purpose as that of any novelist. Long before the Germans walled in the Warsaw Jews, Levinson had begun taking notes from personal observations toward a description of Jewish culture. Before he had begun this task in 1935, he had already published two books, The *Diaspora* and *Customs*. As the content of the published archive makes only too clear, he was engaged in writing a sequel to his scholarly works when the catastrophe struck that gave his work a tragic point.

Levinson is a human being with palpable oddities and weaknesses to go along with his scholarly resolution. He is small and ugly, uncertain of himself in important personal situations that lie outside the compilation of his archive, a lonely man who discovers the meaning of family life in the midst of the ghetto's worst hours. The reader might expect the development of some pronounced personality from the stream of reflections that Levinson showers upon his friends' lives—a delineation of the hyper-curiosity of an arch-journalist—and Hersey certainly accomplishes this. What is far more surprising is that Levinson can also be seen as another ghetto resident, an individualized member of the "family," measurable beside Dolek Berson,

Rachel Apt, Henryk Rapaport, Fischel Schpundt, and the more than fifty characters whom he records with insatiable industry.

Levinson is a true scholar. His method is impeccable, and his curiosity is unlimited. Each of several hundred episodes in *The Wall* begins with the archivist's formal notation: "EVENTS JULY, 1942. ENTRY JULY 12, 1942. N. L." A reason is given for every break in chronological sequence, whether in the events themselves or in their telling. Something that Levinson may have transcribed without comment about one of his friends in a given entry is suddenly followed by the archivist's confession of having misunderstood him. Levinson is his own gloss on occasions much in the manner that Hersey had intended him to be a chorus in interchapters. Yet, each gloss, indeed the persistence of scholarly procedure right up to the moment of leaving the ghetto—itself a moment in which Levinson discovers much about himself that he had not expected to find—adds convincingly to Hersey's most complicated effort at characterization.

At such points, one begins to wonder if Hersey had not chosen a far more difficult way of telling his story than his original plan of omniscience—no matter how personally unqualified he felt for the task. Levinson not only characterizes himself, but he must not permit that self-characterization to hamper the development of such major figures as Dolek Berson and Rachel Apt. They cannot be merely figures observed by the archivist. The reader must instead accept the condition that one may gain from the archive Berson's or Rachel's true estimate of Levinson, or—stretching the mechanism almost to the breaking point—one must accept the archivist's ability to trace in their full intensity the emotional tones of events he did not witness.

Finally, from the miscellaneous volume of his entries, Levinson is also responsible for the narratives which exemplify Hersey's nineteen themes, all of these in meaningful arrangement and weighted according to their importance. Levinson is responsible for the source material which becomes the coherent study of the destruction of the ghetto. "The Editor" (perhaps a device to cover a device) shares this responsibility, of course, but only to the limit that he may cut and paste. The Editor, *in propria persona,* once he has accounted for the archive in his prefatory note, appears only in a few parentheses. With some effort of the will, the reader must remember that the "Levinson Archive," described as a hoax on the copyright page, has, after all, been excerpted and arranged by a latter-day historian, working with translators and guided by reminiscences of Levinson from the ghetto survivors, Rachel Apt and Henryk Rapaport. Levinson, presumably, had no vision of a long novel in six sections.

III *The Story of a Family*

The Wall is the story of the Warsaw ghetto from November, 1939, when German occupation policies began to be enforced, to May, 1943, when the last houses were razed. At the same time, it is the story of a "family" of Jews of various backgrounds who increasingly depend upon one another as their ordeal grows. As in most of Hersey's writing, there is a contest between the prospect of annihilation and the will to live. This conflict is far more complicated in *The Wall* than in *Hiroshima* because annihilation comes to the Warsaw ghetto through a protracted series of decrees and harassments. The will to live is consequently expressed by some Jews as the will to fight, by others in the deviousness of their accommodation, and by a few in their blindness to the possibility of being killed. The will to live also involves the definition of a new way of life, for one of the mounting ironies of this story is that as the Warsaw Jews become more and more literally enclosed by a wall, they lose their submissiveness as a minority and their withdrawal into empty custom—one of the most characteristic marks of the ghetto Jewishness. Hersey, through Levinson, quotes Peretz on this point:

> Now I am not advocating that we shut ourselves up in a spiritual ghetto. On the contrary, we should get out of such a ghetto. But we should get out as Jews, with our own spiritual treasures. We should interchange, give and take, but not beg.
>
> Ghetto is impotence. Cultural cross-fertilization is the only possibility for human development. Humanity must be the synthesis, the sum, the quintessence, of all national cultural forms and philosophies. (550)

Levinson utters these words as he struggles to finish a lecture that is given deep in a bunker crowded with virtually every off-duty resident of the dwindling ghetto. To the extent that the story is about Levinson and a people discovering their identity, this moment is the climax of *The Wall.*

The Wall begins with Levinson's first impressions of Dolek Berson, a man who loves to argue, a man with gusto, a drifter.

They have spent a week as hostages in Pawiak prison, along with other members of the hastily recruited *judenrat*. This experience is their first real taste of the Nazi occupation, and it seems to be something with which they can contend, despite a lingering uncertainty about the full extent of German policy toward Jews and how it will be met. The Warsaw Jews have, of course, heard of the Nazi racial decrees in Germany. Pavel Menkes, the baker, has told Berson that he will fight: "Overt opposition. Kill the rats. Show a fist." But whom would the baker fight, Berson asks: "'Hitler in person? Rosenberg? The S. S. Commander for the Warsaw district? Or some individual German citizen, comply-ing, shaking his head but complying. Or, more availably, a Polish citizen, who didn't seem to heed the decrees. Whom would this baker fight? . . . No, thinks Berson, there is only one re-sistance: it is inward. It is living one's Jewishness as well as possible, meeting things as they come.'"

Both Berson and Menkes are eventually proven correct when Jewishness becomes Resistance, but there are many other re-actions to the inception of German rule. Ghetto community life is highly diversified as Jews of every conceivable background are driven in and scurry about for situations. There are the traditional factions: Zionists, who are almost jubilant with this proven justification for their militancy; Socialists, who cling to the idea of a working-class party that will have strong links with Socialists outside the wall; romantics, who can be attracted by any cause that promises action; and Communists, who are more bewildered than the others because of the virtual impossibility of rationalizing Soviet policy in late 1939. More obvious than these formal groups are simply the *kinds* of people who have begun to encounter their own commitment to being Jews. Some can still think of Sienna Street as "the best kind of neighbor-hood" or believe, as Pan Apt does, that "money would do every-thing." Others, such as Rachel Apt, who becomes the heroine of the novel, must begin living their lives as Jews, trying occa-sionally to "memorize the Polish parts of their lives." Levinson observes amusedly that they are a "small France," these people whom the Germans have blocked off as Jews.

The community responds to the foreshortening of its natural diversity by setting up committees, planning resistance measures whether these consist of evasions by the *judenrat* or plans for eventual fighting. Their children's schooling becomes a form of resistance as do the religious services now conducted in their homes. But in all of these activities of the early months, the ghetto dwellers have been able to ignore the extremity of their plight. Only as the Germans post laws identifying Jews racially and thereby forcing apostates to enter the ghetto, only as Pan Apt finds that money cannot buy his deliverance, and only as German soldiers form cordons at every ghetto exit do the Jews realize that they are locked within their wall.

It would be tedious to summarize in comparable detail—but it is not tedious to read—the remaining five parts of *The Wall*. These sections are organized simply enough on parallel lines of development: first, the progress of the Jews from bewildered individual victims to a compact group of fighters as their numbers dwindle and the ghetto area contracts block by block; second, the growth of a family, as such solitary individuals as Noach Levinson, Dolek Berson, and Rachel Apt develop intense loyalties toward one another. With these sweeping story lines firmly in hand, Hersey writes the novel in as many short episodes as can readily simulate the Levinson archive.

Levinson's point of view is dominant, but it is by no means the only important one. He is not merely a master interrogator, but also a superb listener—indeed, he is so intent upon fidelity to the word and gesture of each conversation that he sometimes misses tones which the reader catches readily. Thus, the reader may recognize Dolek Berson's capacities long before Levinson has ceased to be distracted by his quality as a drifter. While Levinson is not himself committed from the start to a plot line for the archives, he has proceeded to this endeavor from his two scholarly volumes, *The Diaspora* and *Customs*, and from the scholarly method that produced them. He has been a member of an ancient literary and historical tradition of patient accretion and limitless curiosity. Accordingly, in *The Wall*, one is far less aware of a chain of circumstances than of a vivid collection of people captured in revealing actions, all of which are ultimately piled together and packed back into the last moments of judgment. Levinson, for obvious reasons, and Dolek Berson and Rachel Apt, because they survive to the final incident, are the most important of these people; but the novel may be even more memorable for the sharpness with which at least fifty other characters are drawn.

There is Fischel Schpunt, gnarled and wizened, who makes the

Germans laugh at him as he ridicules them. Ben-Levi, a Nobel
Prize winner, grandly shirks leadership up to the moment he
leaves Warsaw with a Uruguayan passport. Rachel Apt's beautiful sister Halinka seems to wither from confinement until she
captures the Zionist leader, Hil Zilberzweig, and undertakes
extremely dangerous resistance missions on her own. The old
socialist, Henryk Rapaport, never quite accepts the fact that his
old Polish comrades have very little concern for the welfare of
the ghetto. Young Schlome Mazur dies as he had lived, rapt in
the spiritual life of his books, the least touched of anyone by the
persecutions. His mother is a remarkable woman whose look at
her dying son is turned suddenly and precisely upon Levinson.
Reb Yechiel Mazur, her husband, is one of many Jews who
must turn from their patriarchal duties to replace Polish janitors
who have left the ghetto apartment buildings. Mordecai Apt
typifies the intellectuals turned laborers, grimly happy that they
are at last being "brutalized for Jewishness." Rabbi Goldflamm
announces that he is burying his Torah:

> —All right (in his natural voice), so we hear that Herr Himmler
> came to pay us a quiet visit last week, *nu*, so what? We heard
> that he visited us last February. Same rumor. But a different feel-
> ing to the goods now. . . . (The rabbi rubbed a thumb and fore-
> finger together, like a tailor trying a cloth.) All right, so we heard
> about the factory for making soap out of Jews in Lublin, we laugh
> and say, "I'll be washing you!" *Nu*, so what, there were supposed
> to be sausage plants with Jewish meat in Tarnopol in March.
> Same kind of foolishness. But I don't know, somehow—. The rabbi
> completed his idea simply by rubbing his thumb and forefinger
> again. . . . So. . . . I am an old loose-tongue, Doctor of Idle Talk.
> Well (and now tears returned to the rabbi's eyes), *nu*, I have de-
> cided to bury my Torah. . . . (254-55)

Wladislaw Jablonski, who had been thrust into the ghetto for
his fraction of Jewish ancestry, poses as a Pole years after he
has been immured. His son, on the other hand, who "must have
been asked questions," is happy with an assured identity. Stefan
Mazur, who works as a policeman for the German-controlled
ordnungdienst, finds himself driven to insure his own survival
by rounding up persons for deportation to the camps ("resettlement quotas"). He must decide at one point, with more vexation
than sorrow, whether to ask his mother or his mother-in-law to
help him by volunteering for the *umschlagplatz*. Fein, the

authentic workman, instructs the Bersons and the Apts in the use and care of tools so that they will not be hauled away as masquerading piano players at the next resettlement call.

Fein adds his own note on the fate of Jews in Eastern Europe: "You see? Last time it was the Russians hated the Jews, and the Germans protected them. Now, the other way around. Maybe that mixes you up? Me: not at all! To me it only means one thing: never trust a *goy* who says he wants to help the Jews. He'll be reaching in our pocket the very next day. So, resettlement! Let them move me around, they'll still hate me! It will serve them right." (287)

There are the barely mentioned *judenrat* officials, Mashkrov and Zweinarca, who become so power driven that they claw their ways to become police chief and "the Jew in charge of deportations." There is Yitzhok Katz, who draws the privileged missions of assassinating them. As this point in the book is reached, near the end of part four, one observes suddenly that no distinction is now made between the Resistance and the Jews, where before Levinson or Berson could speak of the resistance as a separate movement within the ghetto.

Places and isolated episodes are equally memorable. Levinson reports back from an expedition which had the *judenrat*'s reluctant permission to rescue Felix Mandeltort from the *umschlagplatz*:

> In the halls and rooms were people in all states and degrees of humanity and inhumanity. I saw two men, evidently Hassids, but clean-shaven now, having quite a merry theological discussion, hurling quips and quodlibets at each other's head. . . . A group of young people were singing songs of Palestine: songs of arable lands and hard work in the sun. A Jewish boy was selling candies for sums of money that in the old days would have bought glorious pieces of furniture and nicely bound books; who had use for money now? One little man, stripped to the waist, was flexing his muscles before a Junak and wrestling furiously with some water pipes against a wall to show how strong he was and what a mistake it would be to deport him. A young man, who must have belonged to some underground group, shouted: *Fools! You are being taken to death!* A woman spat on him and said contemptuously: *Troublemaker!* Many of the deportees rushed at us and begged with wild eyes for water. I can only say that I was far more terrified by this scene than I was yesterday by the selection. The *umschlagplatz* is Gehenna. It is beyond life. (350)

Brilliantly arranged is the five-page section which begins with a consultation of the dietary laws, followed by the kosher slaughter of an old horse, and, two days later, the "family's" feast, at which "even Rabbi Goldflamm and Reb Yechiel Mazur had violated, without any visible signs of struggle, the prohibition of the Talmud: *A man shall not eat to the fill in time of hunger.*" One also remembers the wedding of Stefan Mazur and Halinka Apt when the groom "pressed gently into the bride's hand, in lieu of a ring, a coin, admissible by ancient custom—not a Polish coin, certainly not a German coin, but (this was Stefan's own idea) a French coin . . . a ten-centime piece, mintage of 1923, but with these values: on one side, the symbolical cap of freedom; on the reverse, the words, in other times so hackneyed, now in the ghetto so rich in meaning: *LIBERTE, EGALITE, FRATERNITE*" (This incident occurs before Stefan hunts down his own people for deportation.) (310).

And there is the crowning incident of the novel when Levinson lectures on the subject of Peretz. This magnificent scene, along with so many of the smaller moments, is a reminder that *The Wall*, for all of the suffering it describes, is at heart a study of human triumph. The novel ends not merely with the destruction of the remaining ghetto blocks, a fact which the escaping Jews scarcely acknowledge, but with the passage to freedom of forty-two men, women, and children. Forty-one actually escape, since Dolek Berson, at the rearguard, pushing more exhausted souls up through the manhole to the street, is left behind when the trucks are spotted by police. From a distance, as they lie inside the moving trucks, Levinson and Rachel Apt hear the firm notes of Dolek's concertina playing *Hatikva*. Since, before this departure, the escapees must wait an unexpected day and a night in the sewers for delayed transportation, Noach Levinson explores the meanings of survival by ceaselessly interviewing his friends:

> We were all talking about one question: What has made our lives worth living?
>
> I asked some amazing questions in those hours, but I never asked that one. No one ever said to me: *This* is what has made my life worth living. Nevertheless, I can see that that was what we were talking about. (609)

According to Rachel Apt, Levinson *entertains* his friends by this questioning but this is far from his purpose. The questions are, of course, an instrument of survival in themselves, as has been the whole Levinson archive. He asks Rutka Mazur Apt of her feelings toward her baby, strangled mere hours before when its cries threatened the group's discovery in a bunker:

N. L. Why are you in such a hurry to give birth to another Jew? Haven't you seen what can happen to Jews?

Rutka: Noach, I'm surprised at you! Can't you see that that is exactly the reason.

The Zionist, Hil Zilberzweig, makes a startling confession: "No I have rebelled only against *excessive* nationalism. The religious zealot ends by being (because of his excesses) anti-religious. In the case of the Jews, the national zealot can likewise become anti-religious—and even, in the consequence of his deeds, anti-Jewish." Levinson banters with Rachel Apt:

Rachel: It is strange. With Dolek, I have never been self-conscious about my face.

N. L. Perhaps your Berson is one of those men who never lets himself have a chance to look at a woman's face. Other interesting features. . . . (626)

Later:

I reminded Rachel that when she first moved into the Jewish section with her family she had had very little experience of inner Jewish life. I asked her to tell me what she thought of this inner life, now that she was on the point of graduating from ghetto-school.

Rachel:—I didn't have as much chance to learn about God; I am rather unclear as to God. But so far as the rest of our religion is concerned, I think there is only one thing: not to hurt anybody. For me the whole of the Torah is in one sentence in Leviticus: Thou shalt love thy neighbor as thyself.

One must love, Rachel persists, even when one's neighbor is a Nazi; for Rachel looks ahead to life beyond the moment of escaping from the ghetto. It is she who is given the last words in the novel, spoken within Levinson's hearing as he bends over in the Lomianka Forest to pluck a leaf from a bush: "—*Nu*, what is the plan for tomorrow?"

This line concentrates vividly what *The Wall* has been all about. While Hersey does not slight either the horror or heroism of the Jewish experience in Warsaw, his overwhelming concern is the study of man's choice of life in the face of death. Life is drawn from the very adversity of menacing death. Life is nurtured on one's history and on the obscure happenings of each day. Life is built on hope for tomorrow and, even more than that hope, on curiosity over what tomorrow will be like. Such a life, as Hersey came to understand it in the long hours with the wire recorder, cannot be simply stated in terms of suffering or heroics, joy or villainy. It is no accident that the effort to define Jewishness is more important to this story than the carefully managed suspense over the fates of individuals. It is equally true that the horror of the German plan for the ghetto is all the greater if the victims are known through their daily lives.

To a great extent, *The Wall*, like *Hiroshima*, is understated because the writer knows perfectly well that such a technique can often be the best way of stating the truth of these great catastrophes. The elaborate index-card system that went into this book does not resemble the construction of the ghetto wall itself, but rather the flowering of community life within the ghetto, which is an erratic growth. Hersey deals with a paradox: as Jews are shoved tighter within the narrowing blocks of their quarter, their lives become much more complicated and expansive. Each person becomes more aware of his growing "family" and its meanings which go beyond the myth of Jewish clannishness or even the tradition of Jewish nationalism. Hersey carefully refrains from forcing the strongest implication of this paradox: that the fruit of the ghetto experience was a pattern for an eventual community of man, a human response to inhuman oppression. For this reason, the book is far better for not having developed individual Nazi characters, inhuman antagonists for the heroes of *The Wall*. A vacillating Pole or a collaborating Jew is enough to illustrate the baser kinds of possible human response to the situation.

IV *Contemporary History and Fiction*

The Wall might have been shorter and more exciting, but Hersey might not have been able to make it so without sacrificing contemporary history. An example of how the story of the

Warsaw ghetto was told differently is Leon Uris's novel, *Mila 18* (1961). Uris had already written the hugely successful *Exodus* about the formation of Israel and was full of the fighting themes of that novel as he began to assemble materials for his version of the events Hersey had covered. (Because Uris has been bloodied relentlessly whenever he has been mentioned by critics, other than a few reviewers, it must be acknowledged that *Mila 18* drew heavily from such strong primary sources as the Ghetto Fighters International House and Shrine, the survivors of the fighting in the Ghetto Fighters Kibbutz and in the International Survivors Association, and the Yad Vashem Memorial Archives in Jerusalem.)[3] Uris also recognized the necessity of an archive device, but he chose not to have the archivist dominate the point of view.

His archivist, Alexander Brandel, contributes a short, italicized "journal entry" before most, but not all, of the chapters. His archives are also buried within the wall before the ghetto is destroyed. This burial, however, is not so elaborate as the one directed by Noach Levinson; but Uris makes the eventual discovery of the cache a more important element of his story. A Swiss newsman is one of the persons entrusted with the secret of their location, and his escape and subsequent vow to return are the climactic action of the story.

In other important respects, one may seize upon the differences between Hersey and Uris, which show why Hersey is a novelist of contemporary history. Uris's archivist is an intellectual leader of the underground by virtue of his skill at plotting and fighting, as well as from the fact that he keeps a journal; he never has time to do anything like deliver a lecture on Peretz, and the omniscient tone of his journals never wavers. Hersey's Dolek Berson was as close as anyone might come to a romantic male lead in *The Wall;* he was a man of interesting contradictions who explained his life to Levinson in those last interviews in the sewers as "having to wait for readiness." His counterparts in *Mila 18* are the Swiss newsman, who has a chance at all kinds of dissipations on the "Aryan side" before returning to his beleaguered friends, and Andrei Androfsky, an *Exodus*-sized Polish Jew, ex-cavalry officer and Olympic soccer player, who is, to put it charitably, an uncomplicated man.

Uris invents distractions that cannot be found in Hersey's novel. The love of Androfsky's life is Gabriella Rak, a beautiful

Roman Catholic, Polish blonde, the daughter of a dead political exile. The Swiss newsman loves Deborah Bronski, beautiful wife of a Jewish turncoat. Neither is like Hersey's plain-featured Rachel Apt or her hare-brained sister Halinka. The only bedroom scenes in *The Wall* are noted in the archives long after they have occurred; *Mila 18* begins with one and places several others in the forefront of the action. Action is often direct and violent in *The Wall,* but it never heightened as it is in *Mila 18.* Again, the archivist merely reports that Yitzhok Katz killed Mashkrov and Zweinarca; but any killing in *Mila 18* is immediate and graphic.

Greater differences between the writers come in their respective treatments of history. Uris, possibly from consideration of his readers, is at some pains to render headline summaries of the European situation to the outbreak of the war. People coming to *Mila 18* from *Exodus* have capsule reminders of Munich, Austria, and Czechoslovakia in Uris's own words as well as in the margins of Alexander Brandel's journal. Events in the ghetto are thus within the constant perspective of an American newspaper reader, who may now in the 1960's, share with Uris an awareness of how deportations from the *umschlagplatz* were contemporaneous with the German defeat at Stalingrad or the first bombings of Berlin. The reader of *The Wall* gets such a perspective through his own calculations: it is enough for Hersey to trace in some detail the private lives of Dolek Berson and Noach Levinson before the war for the reader to know how the people who were to be herded into the ghetto lived before they were struck by the terror. He needs to insert no editorial notes about the 1930's in Europe, nor about the war in the world outside the ghetto.

But this is simply a comparison between one writer to whom contemporary history was already a thoroughly ingrained part of his consciousness and another writer who had to collect material for a novel. They vary more sharply still in understanding and presenting contemporary history as a consequence of the past. Uris is compelled to take several pages for an instant summary of Jewish life since the Diaspora. Levinson enters Hersey's novel with this at hand and merely allows what is relevant of a thousand years' history to escape from his vast inner archives to illuminate whatever he happens to be writing about in the present. Here may be the most powerful instances of what David Daiches called "the miracle of compassion" in Hersey's novel:[4] the writer has so fully entered into the consciousness of the people whom he is writing about that a reader may gain some illusion of the life that Jews must have led within the ghetto. Uris writes devotedly and admiringly of heroic events and only of those events. While the reader may be certain that the devotion and admiration have not been misplaced, this is about the limit of his satisfaction with *Mila 18*, unless he has also read *Exodus*.

The point of all this comparison, however, is not to belittle Uris, but to provide a further means of understanding Hersey's work. To fully extend the comparison requires one to observe that Uris had not been a journalist at the time he wrote *Mila 18*; he was a professional novelist with a background of writing about emphatic characters caught up in violent actions. He approached the historical materials of the Warsaw ghetto full of intense sympathy, but also full of certain fixed conceptions of what made a successful novel of action. He was as theoretical about what would make a good novel as, for example, Norman Mailer was when he went about acquiring the combat infantry experience that would, with his reading as a Harvard undergraduate, help in writing *The Naked and the Dead*.[5] Neither Uris nor Mailer had the problem of discovering form that faced Hersey when he began listening to his wire recordings. The result would suggest that Hersey had strong advantages from having been a journalist and that a journalist may not be utterly handicapped as a novelist of contemporary history.

"A journalist is not allowed to be confused," he wrote some years after *The Wall* was published; "he must *know*."[6] And, if he is truthful and humble, he must write within the limits of what he does know. Such a journalist, however, understands these limits by acknowledging that there is a vast complexity lying beyond them. "Fiction," Hersey wrote further, "is not afraid of complexity as journalism is. Fiction can deal with confusion." These remarks point to the greatest difference between *Hiroshima* and *The Wall:* the report in *Hiroshima* is rigidly restricted to the survivors' accounts against the background of objective information available at the time the article went to press in the *New Yorker* offices; *The Wall* leaps into the complexities of the ghetto struggle and all of Jewish custom that lay behind it. The complexities flow forth in the fragments of the Levinson archives; and any simplification, or any semblance of sure knowledge that may be derived has come cumulatively, has been stated glancingly a thousand times in the midst of fictional circumstances. Hersey has, in fact, overthrown all his professional habits as a journalist to demonstrate that his novel is simply a great instance of a story which, if not eternal, is continuous with the lifeline of all humanity. He records the day, and then he has Rachel Apt ask: "*Nu*, what is the plan for tomorrow?"

CHAPTER 4

Two Novels in Mid-Career

W HILE WORKING on *The Wall*, Hersey had little time for reporting assignments. With the demise of *'47—The Magazine of the Year* just at the turn of the year when that publication was due to have been renamed, he had no formal connection with any magazine. In the late 1940's and early 1950's he contributed a few "profiles" and reports to the *New Yorker*[1]— with President Truman, Bernard Baruch, and Israel as subjects —but otherwise found himself then a full-time writer of fiction. Problems that he began facing as a new novelist are reflected in *The Marmot Drive* and *A Single Pebble*, the sharply contrasting novels which follow *The Wall*. In the first book, an oblique response to contemporary history misfires; but the second is one of the best of the many good short novels that have been produced by postwar American writers. In the 1950's, as Hersey became a settled novelist in suburban Connecticut, few interests drew him from his writing. Whenever he was drawn out, he was most often a citizen supporting a cause.

I   *Engagé*

Hersey acts upon his beliefs, as one may gather from his writing without troubling to check his other activities. He joined the Authors' League of America in 1948; and, instead of merely sticking his new membership card in his wallet, he worked on committees seeking to straighten out problems with copyright and censorship. The trouble with the Allied Occupation Command in Tokyo over publication of *Hiroshima* had given him considerable incentive to do these things. Attacking such problems is characteristic of the man who was, on the other hand, reluctant to discuss a writer's problems in public forum. "It is easier to write about writing than it is to write the sort of writing that ought to be written about," he has said.[2] Although an obvious choice for such engagements, he has not appeared on extended lecture tours, nor has he spent any time as a visiting faculty member at an American university.

In 1950, he was a member of the committee appointed to draft a platform for Connecticut gubernatorial candidate, Chester Bowles. This was his first action as a Democratic Party worker; significantly, he put himself to work rather than merely offer his name. He supported presidential candidate Adlai Stevenson in 1952 through local and professional groups; with John Steinbeck, Herman Wouk, and Cleveland Amory, he reported a "relentless attempt by a majority of the nation's newspapers to play down one candidate." He was the last signer and presumably, therefore, the main writer of a letter to the New York *Times,* questioning the newspaper's endorsement of General Eisenhower in the light of the candidate's alleged concessions to his defeated convention opponent, Senator Taft, on questions of foreign policy.[3] With Allan Nevins, Richard Hofstadter, Max Ascoli, and several others, Hersey held that the Republicans were a "party that, at best, can only give the country a leaderless administration."

He was far more active in 1956 when he served as a speechwriter with the Stevenson campaign entourage. According to New York *Times* writer James Reston, Hersey had been one of a group including Arthur Schlesinger, Jr., and J. Kenneth Galbraith, who in September were "unhappy with the opportunistic, expedient tone of Stevenson's speeches" and wanted him to return to the level of his 1952 campaign.[4] Significantly, Stevenson's speech calling for a nuclear test ban was made after these men joined his campaign and had presumably won their point. The eventual enactment of a test-ban agreement with the Soviet Union may not be traced certainly to this Stevenson speech, much less to any part that Hersey may have had in writing it, but the sheer possibility of there being any connection between Hersey's decision to approach Stevenson in 1956 and the degree of success the test ban has had to date supports Hersey's earlier statements about the value of reinforcing convictions with deeds.

II   The Marmot Drive

The immediate results of his involvements in politics in two presidential election campaigns were not especially reassuring, however. In the grim months after Stevenson's first defeat, when Senator Joseph McCarthy's subcommittee investigations were being intensified, Hersey plunged into the writing of his third novel, *The Marmot Drive*. It was to be a thorough departure from anything he had written, and perhaps his greatest failure.

The story is about Hester, a New York girl on a weekend in a small Connecticut town to visit the parents of the man she thinks she loves. She arrives in time for a woodchuck hunt (the "marmot drive") which brings out all of the fears and weaknesses of the townspeople and a good bit of self-revelation for the young visitor. Her love affair becomes far more complicated than she had supposed, and the worst complication is her attraction to her prospective father-in-law. All of this action is set against a rural New England of lights and shadows loosely reminiscent of Hawthorne's, whose much surer delineation of good and evil is missing. There is just enough resemblance to the moods and settings of some of Hawthorne's tales to establish the fact that Hersey is allegorizing. Or, as is the case with even some of Hawthorne's allegories, it seems that the writer must be writing that way because his story isn't interesting enough in itself. Tunxis is a shabby place as Hester first sees it.

> . . . a dull little station of gray clapboard, hooded by magnificent elms and across the way she got a glimpse of half a dozen store backs, cheaply built structures crowded together with a squalid, tenemental look far out of key with the clean landscape of tilled valleys and traprock cliffs through which the train had come for the second of the two hours the trip from the city had taken; out of key, too, with the image of Tunxis that Eben had induced in her mind, of white houses and a white church breasting a quiet common. The center of Tunxis, she thought with disappointment, was to be after all just another montage of soft-drink signs, tar-paper shingles, gas-station pennants, and grinning billboards; somewhere beyond the stores she supposed she would find a rank growth of television masts, new bulrushes in a dark swamp. (10)

The meanness of man's efforts on New England soil is a controlling feature of the context of this novel, one which overshadows any reader's efforts to idealize the New England character at the expense of New York office workers. The Tunxis villagers are like the human beings whom Robert Frost set down in New Hampshire and the Puritans of William Carlos Williams' *In the American Grain* who survived in their "littleness" at odds with the New World they settled.[5] Any exceptional persons in Tunxis are like Edwin Arlington Robinson's isolates. Worse, when things begin to happen in Tunxis, these villagers behave as meanly and fearfully as other Americans in the security investigations of the early 1950's. It is Hester's privilege to witness all these possibilities on her weekend in Tunxis when her prospective father-in-law, Matthew Avered, becomes the scapegoat of his fellow Tunxians as they spend their energies and anger on the woodchuck hunt. "A Yankee, a real Yankee—well, that's a person who's an idealist even after he's come to see how hopeless life is," Mathew tells Hester. So he speaks for himself; most Tunxians, though, "know how bad things are, but at least keep trying to be decent people" (16-17).

The woodchuck hunt shows the villagers at their worst and Matthew Avered, their Selectman, at his most isolated. It is he who must recognize that an emergency exists when woodchucks infest gardens, overrun Thighbone Hollow, and appear ready to walk right into people's houses. It is he who must remind them that it is a civic obligation to destroy the marmots. He must coax reluctant taxpayers in town meeting and parry the trivial objections to mass action, most of them tinged with personal insult. The restraints upon the decent people of Tunxis are usually most taut when they are faced with someone who tries to be more than merely decent. "As if they resented his intelligence and wanted to destroy him for it," Hester considers.

Everyone is eventually assembled at dawn in four divisions to hunt the pests. Martial order must be maintained even at the expense of separating Hester and young Eben Avered. The girl is, therefore, thrown alone into the bewildering event; she is thus given more opportunity than she can handle to know herself and her fiancé against the backdrop of the people and surroundings from which he came. But her perspective is limited on this hunt. The morning is foggy; and, when the sun breaks through, the air is stiflingly hot. The New England forest becomes an "Equatorial Jungle," especially to a girl who has been spending day after day at a desk on the air-conditioned seventeenth floor of a concrete building in midtown Manhattan. The story of the hunt lurches back and forth in a maze of Hester's impressions with quick alternations of sunlight and dense tree shadows, and sudden appearances of the Selectman; Eben; Anak Welch, the giant; Roswell Coit, the town bully; and Mrs. Tuller, the virago who leads Hester's division. The people who had been reluctant to form the hunt are now impatient to find woodchucks, and the

Selectman's careful strategy of forming divisions and advancing
along determined lines plainly bores them. Woodchucks elude
them entirely the first day.

Frustration is rampant the second day, when the weather turns
warmer and the woodchucks are even more elusive. The Selectman, who persists in exerting his leadership, now becomes more
openly the Yankee idealist who insists on finishing a job and
finishing it well. "You mustn't think that I'm some kind of
Captain Ahab," he tells Hester. "No, no! I only look for good and
bad in people. The drive's just a practical measure" (109). There
still aren't many woodchucks to be found, and most of those that
are seen escape. Some of them bare their teeth before bolting.
A mother woodchuck pushes her young to one side and burrows
into a thicket to save herself, an action which disgusts those who
witness it. The villagers now resent the Selectman's failure to
flush woodchucks even more bitterly than they had opposed him
when he had worked to get the drive underway. As the beasts
escaped them, the Selectman almost becomes the object of the
hunt himself. It would have been a fine time for him to have
found a cluster of the animals, organized a squad of attackers,
and then conducted an effective extermination. However, he is
too complicated a man to have things go so smoothly. He strays
from his purpose just long enough to ruin himself.

From the moment that she first sees him, Hester compares the
Selectman to his son. She senses opposition between them as she
struggles to find likenesses between them. Most of the time she
tries to idealize these differences:

> . . . the father living in the world of stern education, personal reti-
> cence, love of nature; of respect for property, idiosyncrasy, pri-
> vacy, and poetry; of literal horsepower and the slow walk; of
> rigid family life; of frugality and thrift, of the Classics and the
> Bible, of charades and early-to-bed—the son living in a prosy,
> urgent, intrusive world, a world of "realities": of revolution every-
> where, of wars and military preparings and posturings, of fear for
> the future; of cities and science, of jets, reactors, and ultra-high-
> frequencies; of cool rationality and nervous breakdowns; of the
> shifty images of TV; of ads, giveaways, strained budgets, gadgets
> bought on the installment plan; of speeding tickets and drunken
> picnics and sexual frolicsomeness in the small hours. The opposi-
> tion was clear in Hester's mind for only a flash, then she began to
> see that her idea was too simple; there were qualifications and
> shadings and loopholes, for in the father's world there had also

been seething repressions and horrible social injustices, there had
been rationalizations and pretenses and fake decencies smothered
with heavy decor, while in the son's world there were miracles of
progress. . . . (105)

Here is the best writing in *The Marmot Drive*; Hersey is closer
than he will come on any other page of the novel to saying something about the unavailability of traditional standards, wistful
idylls, or the past itself to Americans in the middle years of the
twentieth century. But, there are rumors of the Selectman's girl-
chasing in the past. Perhaps he has been isolated not merely by
his intelligence. Hester remembers how easily and unworthily
she had lost her chastity some months before on a Florida vaca-
tion. At the same time, she receives a few crude attentions from
Rosewell Coit; but rarely during the two-day marmot drive does
she see Eben or hear from him. The habit of comparing him to
his father gradually becomes a matter of chasing the Selectman.
As his fellow townsmen find themselves turning from woodchucks to Matthew Avered as their quarry, so does Hester mark
him for her private pursuit. She tells herself that she wants to
get him alone so that he can help her understand Eben better
(the problem of whether or not to marry Eben was the reason
for the weekend, and she does recall it occasionally); but she
also imagines that the Selectman could wipe out the memory of
her Florida seduction. The idea comes to her when she is alone
in a sun-drenched clearing staring at a woodchuck skeleton:

. . . were you like me? Didn't you stop to think? Did you thrash
around till the toils had you? Not out loud, not even in a whisper,
not even silently did Hester explicitly ask the woodchuck's relics
what it had been like to die in the vines.
But we *are* different, Hester thought. We men and women
think about each other. They'll be back for me. Ha! she let herself complain. When do we think of each other? When we're
afraid, when we need company, when we're afraid of losing something, when we're afraid of death—then we're selfless enough. All
the rest of the time: bellies, genitals, if possible a heel on somebody's else's neck.
And then Hester was thinking how pleasant it would be to be
embraced by Eben's father. Here in the woods. He was experienced, compassionate, and troubled by daydreams; he would be
a hundred times better than the Mandeson, the only one she'd
had. It would be wonderful, she openly thought. Not here in the
snarled vines, of course, but in the soft-floored forest. (126-27)

Hester is largely unaware, in her lustings, of the Selectman's own great struggle throughout the hunt. Not only has he contended with woodchucks and the hostility of his fellow townsmen, but he has been alert to Hester's problem and its new spur to his son's long-standing antagonism. There is always the strong suspicion that Matthew Avered has gone a long way toward contriving his own trial: that he has pursued the marmot drive for a day and a half through every briar in the township on a tortuous route to the copse in the woods where he is finally alone with his son's intended. He knows what she has on her mind, knows his own vagrant capabilities, and knows that there may be some connection between the girl's presence in Tunxis and the confrontation with his fellow townsmen.

They come together by an abandoned church, whose long dead Parson Churnstick had driven parishioners away in his "off-and-on crazy moods." The Selectman, who had backslid from this church when others had left in anger, had come by it alone on a few earlier occasions, once notably to see a woodchuck tottering down an aisle toward the pulpit: ". . . it was spooky; I wasn't born in the woods to be scared by a groundhog, but that gave me a nasty turn—it was one of the things that made me want to go ahead with this drive as soon as folks would cooperate. Church is no place for a woodchuck. I could just picture one of them up in the pulpit giving forth on morality and damnation" (217). Instead of openly flirting with him, an impulse which froths angrily behind Hester's every gesture, she engages the Selectman in a moral discourse. She confesses herself "all mixed up," unable to learn what love is, possibly because the times are against her. Sometimes, she confesses, the Selectman seems to mean more to her than Eben does. What can she believe? she asks him. The Selectman proves no more available as a counselor than he might have been as a lover. Eben and Hester, he declares, "will have to struggle along on whatever leftover ethics they can scrape up."

No city girl should think that she rediscovers old American truths in a New England village surrounded by grinning billboards. There is no sanctuary from what assails her and the rest of the century, or hadn't she noticed what the woodchuck hunt was all about? Predictably, however, once they are both convinced that any peril is removed from their relationship, the Selectman is plunged into real jeopardy. He stops a few hours later to take a speck out of Hester's eye, and this solicitous action is spied upon by Mrs. Tuller. She and everyone else who know that the pair had been together in the abandoned church now find something else to pursue besides the wearisome woodchucks. The creatures got away because the Selectman was dallying with his son's girl. Here at last was something outrageous enough to bring the Selectman to trial. He is arraigned with dispatch, and "a light public whippin'" is decreed. Woodchucks actually appear on the edge of this gathering and then slip away as the sentence is pronounced. The townspeople fetch a board, rope, and whip; and the compassionate giant, Anak Welch, the most reluctant person at hand, is appointed to do the scourging. The Selectman makes no protest; he merely checks the legality of the punishment with the Town Counsel. Everyone except a silent Hester is satisfied that the punishment squares with tradition. Once it is over, the Selectman returns to the woodchucks in the hollow; but this time he faces them alone. Desperately and grotesquely, he stumbles around killing fifteen of the animals, while his fellow townsmen look on laughing.

But the novel has been told from Hester's point of view, and she is now witnessing events she is supposed to have caused. The Selectman is being whipped for her sake. Is there nothing she can do to prevent this anachronistic punishment? Privately, she denies any mistreatment by the Selectman, but neither Mrs. Tuller nor Eben believes her. As she watches each development leading to the Selectman's scourging, she is determined to shout out his innocence; but she remains silent. As she stays silent, she is overcome by suspicion herself: "Besides (what a confused and mean comfort!) why was the Selectman so passive? Was he really somehow guilty of something?" (261). The point of the novel is thereby complete. Terrible as the public whipping may be, it is as bad to say nothing in the face of such an outrage. Hester leaves Tunxis, as confused as ever about marrying Eben Avered; she knows only that the marmot drive has changed her forever, whether she marries him or not.

III   *Bad Reviews*

It is difficult to decide what *The Marmot Drive* is about apart from its own unclear story. Hersey describes something like the behavior of nations seeking scapegoats to blame for their own frustrations. Yet this scapegoat is the man who initiates the search. The Selectman stands for no clear type of victim however he may suggest several historical individuals. At one point it is said that he is resented because of his intelligence; at another, because of his compassion. If one could ignore the Selectman's actions, it might be possible to suggest some parallel with Adlai Stevenson, whose wit and urbanity may have contributed to his defeat in the 1952 election. But what sort of woodchuck hunt did Stevenson set in motion? It would be as profitable to see Harry Truman in the Selectman, determined to drive woodchucks beyond the 38th parallel, and then being condemned for not bombing them beyond the Yalu. This would leave Hester and her problems more of a mystery than ever, except that, in any case, she is guilty of moral cowardice for being the one person who recognizes the victim's innocence and virtues and fails to speak up for him.

Very generally, of course, Hersey does present a familiar situation worked over by many earlier novelists and one toward which almost any American social novelist might turn: what should realists proclaim as their creed once the old idealism has been rejected? The people of Tunxis also might be contrasted to the fighters of the Warsaw ghetto; in the petty trial of the Americans, they fall apart very easily. That part of their tradition that respected human tenacity is forgotten. They cling to the whipping post.

Reviews of *The Marmot Drive,* almost uniformly unfavorable, went far toward stigmatizing Hersey as a journalist incapable of writing non-journalistic fiction. Neither the reviews nor the writing of the novel itself, however, had any damaging effect on his development as a writer. Neither diminished his interest in the world around him, and, therefore, the basis of his career lay intact. World peace, American politics, and man's will to survive continued to interest him as much as fictional technique and far more than any self-conscious image of a novelist's career. He had, besides, unsettled questions such as the meaning of what he had rediscovered in China (something he had not been able to work into the *Life* and *New Yorker* articles), or what men really thought about fighting a war (more than what Hersey had been able to jot down in interviews).

Something that proved almost nothing about Hersey's fame or prospects was his election to the National Academy of Arts and Letters in 1953. At thirty-nine, he was the youngest writer ever to have been chosen for this honor. Two others elected at the time were E. E. Cummings and Roger Sessions.

Through the middle 1950's, between presidential elections, Hersey became increasingly interested in education. Although he was the product of private schools, he was one of the working members of the National Citizens' Commission for the Public Schools, a group organized in 1953 to study all aspects of the public schools (school plants as well as curriculum and teaching methods) and to make recommendations for action by government authorities. He was no "letterhead" member, but devoted many hours to visiting classrooms, working with local committees, writing reports, and finally organizing a National Citizens' Council for the Public Schools. He was active with these organizations until they disbanded in 1959, and a comprehensive statement of his position on educational questions may be found in "Intelligence, Choice, and Consent," a pamphlet published by the Woodrow Wilson Foundation. The full fruit of these pursuits appeared, of course, in *The Child Buyer* (1960).

During the same years, he continued work on behalf of writers' organizations. As head of the Authors League Commission on Censorship, he reported in 1955 that censorship had been more widespread in the past two years than at any time in the previous two decades. In December, 1955, he was named a member of the Authors Guild Council of the Authors League. It may be significant that Hersey's self-awareness as a writer was expressed by these activities rather than by lectures and essays on writers' problems.

IV A Single Pebble

In June, 1956, he published *A Single Pebble,* a very short novel that is as lucid as *The Marmot Drive* had been obscure. *A Single Pebble* is the story of what an unnamed American hydraulic engineer learns as he travels up the Yangtze on a junk. The engineer tells his story retrospectively of a time when he "and the century were in their twenties," and he was full of an ambitious plan to dam the Yangtze River and solve the gravest economic and technological problems of the Chinese people. He had a typically Western approach to the task. So convinced was he of the benefits they would receive that he felt that he needed only to inform the Chinese of his plans for the dam to rise as quickly as modern machinery would permit. Misery and backwardness would vanish on the spot—or so the engineer thought all the way across the Pacific from San Francisco until he left his Shanghai hotel room to board a steamer going upriver.

The first thousand miles of passage left him unbearably impatient: endless miles of smooth, brown water cutting through brown plains all the way up to Ichang, the last river port before the gorges begin. Further passage upriver from this point is by junk, or, to be perfectly accurate, by trackers, those coolies taken aboard by junks at Ichang, who will be put ashore at all further points where the current or the narrowness of passages between rocks may require the vessel to be pulled upstream. Understanding nothing of the implications of this further mode of travel, the engineer had finally arrived at the starting point of the search for his dam site.

He boarded his junk before dawn one morning, only to wait the rest of the day and all that night before the vessel pushed off at the next daybreak. For twenty-four hours (his measurement, no one else's in Ichang) he was "held in a prison of others' patience." The ship's cook spent all of the waiting day ashore ostensibly to buy some white cabbages, but he returned at night without any cabbages, yet in triumph carrying several chickens by their necks. No one seemed to mind, not even the junk owner, who stood to lose money by any delays. The engineer, for all of his continuing impatience, was not at all surprised by what he saw since it confirmed all the stereotypes of Oriental backwardness that he had brought along with him from the States.

Confined in idleness as a junk passenger, however, he was forced then and in the slow days immediately following to lower his vision from the chimerical dam to the human beings who shared the deck with him. He began learning about the river people before beginning to learn about the river itself. Four distinct personalities began to emerge from among the Chinese surrounding him: the owner, the owner's wife, the head tracker, and the cook. Individuals stood out from among the other trackers only in fleeting moments of danger when they were at work, or of folly when they were resting.

The owner appeared to be the most solitary figure of the lot. He was like the Western ship's captain in this solitude, but he seemed to lack some of the captain's functions and prerogatives. During a tracking operation, he is as frustrated as the engineer;

the trackers' movements were so instinctively geared to the head tracker's cries that the owner down on the conning deck could only wave or shout to please himself. He was apathetic toward any consideration of speed or profit, but he was perfectly aware that his existence was determined by speed and profit. He may be the one whose position with respect to the river was the most ironic: he was damned by his entrepreneurial role even though he realized as keenly as anyone else (even as keenly as the tragic head tracker) the precarious hold that a man floating on a junk has upon the Yangtze. No one aboard was less interested, therefore, in the engineer's dream.

The owner's wife, who was very young, was exceptionally important to the story. Her whole life was a little like the engineer's first frustrating day aboard the junk. She was completely committed to her role as wife and servant to the owner; but, at the same time, she was deeply in love with the head tracker. Her only shipboard duty was to make her husband comfortable. She had more time than anyone else to converse with the engineer and was apparently not at all overcome by the novelty of a foreign passenger. The engineer, on the other hand, hardly knew what to make of her. Except for her wide-open eyes, her appearance was not striking. Her conversation, usually simple, was sometimes grudgingly undertaken; but she occasionally became a "well of understanding and learning." Certainly, she was a well of river lore and marvelously retained volumes of poetry by heart. She was the engineer's guide to the river, but she was so passive that she did not even figuratively take him by the hand along its banks and into its depths. He had to listen very closely, continually check his impatience, and, more, subdue his own desire to seem prepossessing in her eyes. His whole vision of a Yangtze valley redeemed by his dam had to be told to Su Ling hour after hour, and only by slow stages could the engineer learn, through her gentle replies, of the horror which such a vision conveyed to the people whom he would help.

The head tracker, known as Old Pebble, was a comparatively young man, nearer Su Ling's age than the owner's. He personified the impossibility of the dam ever being built. He might strike the observer at first as the traditional human beast of burden because his job was to pull harder on the ship's lines than any of the trackers he had. Once the tracking began, he was literally tied in his lines, not to be released until the passage over rapids or through narrows was secured. It was at first inconceivable to the American engineer that Old Pebble could have any attachment to his job. He catechized Old Pebble: What does he do? He pulls a towline. What is his future? He has very little. What are his goals? In his spare time ashore he drinks wine. What does he want? He will stay on boats because there will always be someone to hire him; and, when he dies, all of his brothers in the boatmen's guild will help pay for his funeral. And the engineer reflected: "I thought that he might be dramatizing himself as a poor, pure-hearted wanderer, one of Heaven's minstrels, to me, a foreigner who asked questions. I could not imagine that a young, vigorous, and cheerful man could live without distant goals: wealth, family, and a name widely known" (14).

Compared to the other three Chinese characters, the cook was ignoble. He delayed the passage by his errand to the market. He sang or shouted antiphonally to the trackers' rhythm. He quarreled with Old Pebble or joked with him. He was aware of all the dangers and hardships of the upriver passage and insultingly indifferent to them. He was cynical about everyone's motives, including his own; but he participated in the sacrifice of a rooster to propitiate the river god. His behavior was impudent and irrational.

The point of the first section of the novel, "The Junk," was that the passive perversity of these people exactly foreshadowed what the engineer would discover about the river itself. These people are unchangeable—and are no different from other individuals who have done the same tasks for several centuries. The junk itself is patterned after a design three thousand years old. It will always require trackers to get it upstream. Why, indeed, does the steamboat line end at Ichang?

The remaining three sections follow a plot suggested by their headings: "The Rapids," "The Dam," and "The Path." In "The Rapids," the action describes the junk being borne through a mad passage of the river by Old Pebble's daring and skills. Yet he and Su Ling believe that because the river had been propitiated by a sacrifice, it had yielded to those who loved it.

The engineer saw exactly what any other Western witness would see: The tracker, in a moment of apparent indecision and weakness, grabbed a loose towline with a bamboo pole and pulled down on it, showing the way for twelve other trackers, who pulled down with him until the biased leverage of the towline's new purchase pulled the junk around in its channel and permitted it to nose its way upstream. "Ayah, this river is a turtle," Old Pebble said contemptuously later on.

He went further in his pride, however; and it remained for the engineer to be driven reckless by his feat. Matching the tracker's boasts, the engineer claimed that he could so change life on this river with twenty thousand dollars that no junk would ever be wrecked and there would never be any need for trackers. Fortunately, for the moment, he said this only to Su Ling. Nothing can change the Great River, she replied calmly. Although she would be marked for the rest of her life by having heard such an impious suggestion, she knew that it would be infinitely worse—fatal—for such a boast to reach Old Pebble. The engineer listened politely enough to her remonstrance, but not well enough to remember.

Old Pebble's action stirred the engineer's ambition. Incredibly enough, the skill and strength displayed in that one heroic moment, which might conceivably have proven to the dullest "foreign devil" that man and the river had wrung a compact from a confrontation stretching over millennia, provoked instead such humanitarian sentiment as might have occurred to the most patronizing philanthropist: ". . . as the days passed, and as I began to see what a dam could mean to the human beings on the boat on which I was travelling, particularly to the trackers, the dam became more important to me than it had been when I had approached it as something theoretically and technically desirable, as an abstraction in a company memorandum and in the minds of some faraway engineers" (91-92).

The junk entered Witches' Mountain Gorge, "the longest, most beautiful, and most mysterious of all the chasms of the river." For twenty miles the river was narrowed to a passage sometimes as small as a hundred and fifty yards across. Here, the river had worn its way over the ages through rock mountains, "which rose vertically from the water for hundreds of feet, then, falling back at knee-, hip-, and shoulder-terraces, rose again, and again, and again, all but perpendicular, until, seen through sudden clefts, they reached craggy pinnacles."

In Witches' Mountain Gorge the trackers worked more arduously, the dangerous nature of their labors varying almost hourly. Witches' Mountain Gorge was plainly, trip after trip, the great test of Old Pebble's life. He was never happier, nor ever more reflective, than in the days he worked and the nights he rested from leading his men over the gorge's rocks and along its narrow towpaths. Once, when a very young tracker slipped into rough water and cried out in pain as his foot became wedged between rocks, Old Pebble leaped gruffly and instantly to his side to free him.

This action, yet another proof of Old Pebble's indomitability, struck the engineer as a sympathetic action like his own suppressed dream. Feeling nearer to the man, near enough possibly to make him hear the message that was all but suffocating him, the engineer found Old Pebble alone on the deck one day repairing a parrel. He complimented him on his handiwork and found him wary. Blind to this unexpected response, he was driven to remark that a bronze-and-wood pulley would be a hundred times more efficient means of holding a towline, but he forgot the Chinese word for pulley, and needlessly spoke instead of how Western engines dwarf manpower. "This thing was not made to be looked at," the tracker said grimly, shaking the parrel in the engineer's face. He left, and moments later the word for pulley occurred to the engineer.

The next day the engineer saw the site for his dam:

Between those two sheer cliffs that tightened the gorge a half-mile upstream, there leaped up in my imagination a beautiful concrete straight-gravity dam which raised the upstream water five hundred feet; much of its curving span was capped by an overflow spillway controlled by drum gates and tube valve outlets, and a huge hydraulic jump apron designed to pass unprecedented volumes of water stood ready to protect both the dam and the lower countryside against the freshets of springtime. Ingenious liftlocks at either side carried junks up and down on truly hydraulic elevators. The power plant was entirely embedded in the cliffs on both sides of the river. The strength of the Great River, rushing through the diversion tunnels that had been used for the construction of the dam, and through other great tubes and shafts bored through solid rock, and finally into the whirling gills of nearly a hundred power units, created a vast hum of ten million kilowatts of light and warmth and progress flowing through high-hanging wires over six widespread provinces. Away through pipelines flowed, too, unimaginable numbers of acre-feet of water, irrigating lands that after the harvest would feed, let me say, seventy-five million Chinese. A terrible annual flood, now making up as the river rose toward its high water level, was leashed in advance by this beautiful arc. Beyond the tall barrier, junks sailed forward with their wares, to Chungking and farther, as on a placid lake. (107-8)

In such a vision all caution vanished, and with prudence went the precious learning the engineer had been granted by Su Ling and Old Pebble. The engineer was driven by his Western demons of technology to tell the girl and the tracker about his dam exactly as he had seen it. He forgot Su Ling's plea never to speak to Old Pebble of changing the river. Every detail of his dream spilled out to the limit of his Mandarin vocabulary and the range of his gestures. More was added. Rapids, whirlpools, currents would be all done away with to everyone's everlasting benefit; with these perils gone, there would be no more pilots, no more tracking. Past any sensitivity in his raving, the engineer was surprised at Old Pebble's reaction. The tracker stood erect in full fury, as if to strike the American; and he turned abruptly to Su Ling and the cook and began to speak in another Chinese dialect. At that instant, the engineer was willed out of shipboard existence. If he would suggest that trackers be done away with altogether, he must himself be obliterated by Old Pebble.

Yet, to the engineer's even greater surprise, he was spoken to amiably enough the next morning. Su Ling related more Yangtze fairy tales, and the tracker added his own gloss from time to time. They stood together, the engineer in the middle, to watch repairmen lash a loose spar. There was some jostling, and a little while later the engineer discovered that his pocket watch was missing.

The engineer's dilemma was extreme at this point. Someone had stolen his watch and had chosen this odd moment of reconciliation in which to steal it. Any of the repairmen or the other deckhands might have stolen it, but no one of them could be singled out as a suspect or was even known to the engineer as an individual human being. Su Ling and Old Pebble denied having stolen the watch and ridiculed the possibility of anyone's having stolen it. The engineer easily imagined that Old Pebble took it as the only token of the engineer's machine-worship, the amulet of his accursed dam. Old Pebble ingeniously ridiculed watches and questioned whether the engineer ever had a watch. He suggested that the junk owner, Old Big, a man who put some value on commodities, might have taken the watch.

Old Pebble's manner was a study for the engineer; he did not know whether it connoted mockery, bluff, or arrogance. Su Ling's face was plainer. Terror-stricken the day before when the engineer had revealed his vision of the dam, she became further terrified and now was also angry over his accusations. It was she, not Old Pebble, who called the engineer a "foreign devil" and sealed his ostracism with this exclusive epithet. She and Old Pebble, of course, realized, as the engineer could not, that these two exchanges on successive days came just before the approach to Wind-Box Gorge, the last and most dangerous passage of the journey upriver to Wanhsien. Both had more than vague premonitions of the tracker's destruction.

Cast off in a corner of the deck by himself, the engineer was made the silent, reflective witness of the junk's passage through Wind-Box Gorge. What he saw was the culmination of all the river fables and hints of river knowledge that had come to him on the voyage; and, along with them, was the final answer to his dream of a dam.

The haul began with "errands of superstition." Ceremonial papers were burned, and bells and pennants were run up on the halyards. Old Pebble handed Su Ling a pair of earrings to "keep the boat dry." Even Old Big permitted himself the gesture of bringing his clenched fists together and bowing to Old Pebble, his "Noise Suppressor." Old Pebble said to Su Ling: "The fruit blossom will have her petals shaken today." Su Ling replied, "The strong branches also tremble when the petals shake." They smiled at what appeared to be self-conscious mockery of high-toned speeches, but they were tense at this moment of the tracker's departure for the path. Within minutes, they entered the lower end of the gorge where, within a dozen boat lengths, there was a visible rise of nearly a foot in the water level. Old Pebble began to lead the tracking songs as the junk was hauled inch by inch uphill. His tone seemed to have become so urgent that even the engineer and the owner began to have the forebodings that have assailed Su Ling since the first mention of the dam. The junk shivered harder and creaked louder than it had at any other point in the voyage.

When the junk reached a relatively easy middle span in the gorge, and the owner and Su Ling turned to a game of "stones"—one that was broken whenever a sudden lurch of the junks causes the bells to ring and the owner to leap up with imprecations against the river. The owner disclosed offhandedly that this trip would be Old Pebble's last haul before he retired to a farm. He had not actually informed the owner of such an intention, but the owner claimed to have had no difficulty surmising it. The engineer (always coming back from being left out of Chinese conversations) impulsively contradicted him. One surmise seemed as good to him as another, and he was shocked by Old Big's angry questioning reply: "What do *you* know about the river?" The man of commodities was no less certain about the river than were the poets, Su Ling and Old Pebble. It was just as monstrous to Old Big as it had been to them that an American could presume to lift a mountain and set it in the middle of a gorge; moreover, he could support his fancies with nothing more than details about unimaginable machines. And, as Old Pebble had done the day before, Old Big cut off the engineer by resuming his talk about the tracker.

With this news, just before the perilous climax is reached, the engineer had the troubling new consideration of people having enough of the river and simply going away from it after years of submitting to its inclemency. He was as far from understanding trackers at this point as he was in Ichang. After all the hazards of daily routine, all the ritual of propitiation, all of a working life spent believing in the river's least lore, a day could come when they simply would have enough and go away.

Suddenly, the junk arrived at the dangerous place. The engineer saw evidence of a crude technology that mocked his dam: a hand-cut path along the face of a cliff, a path which had "a ceiling, an inner wall, and a floor of solid rock, with only peril for an outer wall." The path was a thousand years old, and its age merged with its terrifyingly small shape to reveal to the engineer, as nothing else had before, the unbridgeable distance between the Chinese and himself. "How could I span a gap of a thousand years—a millennium in a day?" he asked himself. Perhaps not with a dam. Patience, beyond any that he could comprehend, had cut the corridor to which the trackers above him clung. He continued to himself: "Suppose I had been called upon to cut stone on a path like this for fifty years of my life, to be relieved then by my son? What if I had been called upon to haul a junk through this path all my life?" (139-40). And as these considerations overwhelmed him, he finally noticed that the path had been cut just wide enough for a tracker leaning on his halter with all his might but not high enough for him to stand straight.

The complete image offered the engineer was overpowering at that moment: all of time and all of the rushing Yangtze, from the snows of Tibet to the brown water off the mainland, drawn through the needle-eye of the gorge, itself threaded year by year by patient trackers. It should have been enough to dash his ambitions forthwith, but the calamitous path was carved only on one side of the gorge. Facing it was a surpassing wonder which became known to the engineer as he detected a sudden change in Old Pebble's facial expression and noticed the tracker's intent glance up the face of the opposite cliff. There, rising from river level to the top of a seven-hundred-foot perpendicular cliff was a pattern of square holes that had been cut with hammer and chisel by soldiers of the Eastern Kingdom when their ships had been trapped in the gorge. Here was patience again, the engineer discerned; but beyond it there was an almost incredible aspiration. At that instant, it seemed to be of the utmost importance to him to fix Old Pebble's face in his mind and to listen to the exact timbre of his song:

> Then Old Pebble broke into the most amazing song I had ever heard from him; a whirling, spiraling, soaring sound of pure joy. It seemed to me to be wordless. He was pulling now with all his strength; he held an arm reaching forward, as if that would hurry him. Still he looked across at the marks on the reddish cliff.
> . . . His face bore a look of great happiness or great pain—much like the faces of people caught in photographs of terrible disasters, their mouths drawn by agony into seeming smiles. His song was thrilling. He strained wildly at his harness. (145)

And at that moment, Old Pebble lost his footing and fell flat forward. The trackers behind him inched ahead; the first to reach him pushed his ankles aside. Old Pebble screamed as he tried to loosen the sennit encircling him so that he could get out of their way. It would not give, and he fell off the edge of the path. For frozen moments, the tracking gang strained at its ropes with Old Pebble suspended ten feet below them and twenty feet above the river. The owner was anxious for his cargo; and, for the safety of all concerned, the junk could not stay long in the gorge. Su Ling was downcast. The cook continued to peel turnips without looking up. The engineer wondered if something in Old Pebble's mind (the dam or the soldiers' ladder) had caused him to fall. Then there was frantic action as the owner screamed for any tracker with a knife to cut Old Pebble's sennit so that the junk could keep moving.

Su Ling moaned inconsolably, but only the engineer refused to accept Old Big's decision: ". . . I felt a desperate love of life, of my own life, and I watched the slow gnawing of the bamboo hawser up there. If that was a minute, it was a very long one. It made me come close to sensing the meaning of the most awesome concepts: paralysis, burial, infinity" (154). He argued with Old Big, but the knives continued to saw at the rope strands; Old Pebble was quickly cast adrift. Mourning and reflecting, the engineer hardly noticed Old Big leap into a sampan and cut loose to attempt to recover his tracker, though he knew the effort would be hopeless.

Getting through the rest of the gorge was anti-climactic, nothing that the engineer would ever remember. The lone remaining puzzle for him was the attitude of the turnip-peeling cook, who took up the tracking chant the moment Old Big had gone over the side after the disappearing tracker. Clues, if any, came from the man's certainty that the owner was alive as certainly as the tracker was dead. The owner had been in a boat, and the tracker had been in the river; that was enough to know. And the owner did, indeed, return, filthy and wet, to interrupt and disperse a banquet provided for the crew by the engineer once they have reached Wanhsien. He brushed aside the engineer's thanks by demanding more money for the trip, as if he were an angry ricksha boy. The engineer paid and the story ends.

A Single Pebble, Hersey's most skillful combination of purpose and technique, is a beautifully written short novel. The writer exploits the superficial simplicity of his materials: a conflict of understanding between the engineer and a carefully limited set of Chinese characters, the cramped junk and the constricted river squarely in the center of a suggested continent that goes from the Himalayas to Shanghai, the measured upriver stages of the plot, the limited range and tone possible for his characters in this situation. *A Single Pebble* stands vividly beside his earlier achievement, *The Wall:* a single enduring memory never to be fully plumbed is set beside the ingenious accretion of testimony which is Levinson's archive.

In *A Single Pebble*, Hersey writes very simply about the need of people to understand one another. Belying the naïve programs

which he had set forth in *A Bell for Adano* and his advice to UN
supporters, he states that human progress cannot spring from
fond hopes alone. *A Single Pebble* may be his truest novel of
contemporary history because it contains his surest vision of
history. The engineer cannot build his dam until the gap of a
millennium has been breached in a day. Yet, he may persist in
his ambition because, despite their technological backwardness,
comparable aspirations have moved these Chinese trackers who
spurn his help. Their history is made up of inhuman patience,
as the hand-hewn path demonstrates; but it also includes the
incredible cliff-ladder on the other side of the gorge. If the
story is taken allegorically, one may read into it a further lesson
of *Hiroshima*: To overcome the immeasurable at its inception,
the atomic age must proceed by equal impulses of patience and
aspiration toward whatever good it may bring mankind.

CHAPTER *5*

The War Lover

Rolling home, rolling home,
Rolling home across the sea,
Rolling home to dear old England,
Rolling home, dear land to thee.

—from "Across the Sea"

A NOVEL about American bombing crews based in England, *The War Lover* was written fourteen years after Hersey had submitted his last dispatches as a *Time-Life* correspondent in World War II. A review of his wartime writing suggests why he waited so long to write his war novel. Although full of the meaning of certain contemporary events in 1943, *A Bell for Adano* had deliberately avoided exploring the meaning of war. Forced by deadlines and other editorial demands to say more about war than he could possibly know, Hersey had written sincerely enough about courage and endurance, combat efficiency and off-duty humanity, as he had seen them and often only as he heard of them. He had copied out carefully the formal statements of motivation and aspiration that came from the men he met, knowing how perfunctory many of these statements were and how his subjects usually left their deeper considerations unspoken. Unavoidably, he had rationalized some of the disturbing facts he came across. He had taken great pains to try to explain the hatred that American soldiers alleged they felt toward the Japanese (always "Japs" in the dispatches) and why it was necessary for American bomber crews to limit their imagination when they went on their missions. In Sicily he had learned about General Patton; and, although he had used only a fragment of the general's legend in *A Bell for Adano,* it had led him to the first suggestions of an altogether different kind of warrior. Patton had come closer than anyone else within his reporter's acquaintance to personifying a love for war, not only when he shot mules but even when he wrote poems. In that first novel, however, Hersey had been incapable of seeing General Patton as more than an undemocratic anachronism, whether in the liberation of Europe or in the world after the war.

Two years later, he made his investigations in the ruins of Hiroshima. The peace cries which he had uttered in *A Bell for Adano* were nothing beside the conviction that swept over him at the site of a hundred thousand instant fatalities. To what he had seen of the enemy's calculated inhumanity in Eastern Europe, he could add the inhuman detachment in the act of one bomb dropped from one plane creating the greatest imbalance in history between the killer and the number of his victims—absurdly hyperbolic war. Nothing he had written about war-making made any sense in the light of this new evidence. Some of these earlier words might have indeed mocked him as he walked through the Hiroshima ruins: "American fliers are not cruel or insensitive, far from it. Most of them are naturally gentle, kind, and generous. If they do not talk much about the damage they do, it is because their job is impersonal. It has to be. . . . The war will end sooner for aviators, and their scars will heal quicker, if they can concentrate coolly on hitting the enemy carefully and well."[1]

He had not written such lines dishonestly or, within the limits of his experience, incompetently. He had simply touched upon one side of a dilemma that he would be years in resolving. Most men that he had met in the war theaters had made war and loved, had killed and yet loved life. A horrifying few of them had seemed to make war and kill without the slightest consideration of the phenomenon of living. The greater number had been pressed into situations where they made war and killed in spite of their natural reverence for life—others' lives, as well as their own. But for some years Hersey postponed following out these observations. *Hiroshima* and *The Wall* set forth concretely the two greatest catastrophes of World War II, the implications of the theme he would struggle with in *The War Lover*. An end to hatred and a beginning to understanding, along with an admiring evaluation of man's will to survive, came from the grim and heroic images of his second and third books. He had not been ready then to consider war-loving and the combat-born love of life as themes for fiction.

The old chantey which stands at the head of this chapter cannot be found in *The War Lover*, but it corresponds well to the life-turning impulses of Lieutenant Charles Boman, co-pilot of *The Body,* at the end of the novel as he crash-lands his stricken Flying Fortress into the English Channel, while his pilot, Buzz Marrow, lies in another part of the ship, stupefied by his fears. Throughout the weeks of their tour in England and during the hours of this present raid, Boman has learned and reflected upon certain discoveries about himself and his pilot. Slowly he has come to realize that Marrow is a war lover and that he himself is a life lover. In the course of the novel, which goes back and forth from the tour to the raid, Hersey minutely traces how each man has become so defined. In the characterization of Buzz Marrow, Hersey has created what one critic has called a superior study of "erotic war motivation,"[2] and perhaps Marrow may be a more interesting psychological study than Boman. On the other hand, Hersey has made his narrator, the short, sensitive co-pilot, one of the most unusual heroes of American war fiction.

The relationship between Marrow and Boman is a little like that between Nick Carraway and Jay Gatsby, except that Marrow protects an ugly auto-erotic fantasy born of fear, while Fitzgerald's hero holds to an incorruptible dream. And Boman does not survive *his* title character, Marrow, in order to retreat to some place where "people will be at a moral attention forever"; instead, he climbs aboard a British rescue launch to return to life and the love of a British girl named Daphne. Boman is almost an anomaly among fictional war heroes in this century for raising such terms as "idealism," "dignity," "decency," and "selfless love" in his thoughts about himself in wartime. For him, at least, the verdict of the lost generation about war and its aftermath has been refuted; and, unlike Hemingway's Lieutenant Henry, he has not seen certain abstractions made meaningless by their reiteration. Observing this man's struggle not to be victimized, but to triumph, may lead one to wonder if Hersey had really advanced beyond his high-minded reportage—or it may raise the corresponding question of whether the bulk of war fiction, other than *The War Lover,* is too negative. Or one might merely doubt that a man should be able to proceed from writing about Hiroshima and the Warsaw ghetto to produce a novel about an idealistic airman.

While the study of Buzz Marrow does indeed contribute to an understanding of the peculiar cruelties of World War II, the characterization of Charles Boman does not compromise this real view of the war. Many readers may appeal from fiction to their own experience to cite World War II combatants who found reasons for being in the war or who became more sentient human beings for having thought deeply about life and death. But such an effect does not make war less terrible or indicate that its sordid aspects have ever been effaced. Idealism in World War II fiction has appeared in several unlikely places, in James Jones's *From Here to Eternity* and *The Thin Red Line*, as well as in such more deliberately turned novels as Irwin Shaw's *The Young Lions* and Herman Wouk's *The Caine Mutiny*. Robert E. Lee Prewitt, of *From Here to Eternity*, met his death by trying to return to his company despite all that happened to him in the stockade. James Jones, ten years later in *The Thin Red Line* is avowedly anti-romantic, but *not* altogether ironic in the dedication to his second war novel: "This book is cheerfully dedicated to those greatest and most heroic of all human endeavors, WAR and WARFARE; may they never cease to give us the pleasure, excitement, and adrenal stimulation that we need, or provide us with the heroes, the president and leaders, the monuments and museums which we erect to them in the name of PEACE."[3]

John Hersey, in fact, draws someone entirely recognizable in Charles Boman, a type of person who is rather arbitrarily ignored in such works as Norman Mailer's *The Naked and the Dead* or John Dos Passos' *Three Soldiers*. There are still mistaken assumptions that *The Naked and the Dead* is the definitive novel of World War II or that the attitudes from *Three Soldiers* and Hemingway's *A Farewell to Arms*, however convincingly presented, were themselves definitive. In Hersey's war novel, as in his other fiction, he works straightforwardly against the grain worn deep by his peers.

The War Lover is developed along two lines of narrative in alternating chapters: "The Raid," which covers the twenty-fourth mission of *The Body* from the moment Charles Boman wakes up to his final rescue from the English Channel; and "The Tour," which turns back to earlier missions and to all the episodes throughout their duty in England which have led Boman to understand his pilot and himself. This structure sometimes makes the raid seem thinly strung out as when an eleven-page "Raid" chapter is abruptly followed by twenty pages of exposition from "The Tour." Such is the complexity of character motivation in *The War Lover* that the exposition, in all, is twice as long as the present action. At its best, however, Hersey's plan provokes suspense and enhances the development of his themes. The whole story is told by Boman in the first person.

Boman has good reason to be up one hundred and thirty-five minutes early on the morning of his fateful mission. It is utterly unlike any of the twenty-three missions that he has flown before. He knows something about his pilot that is not merely disquieting for the success of a mission—the safe return to England. This knowledge imposes the greatest possible strain upon his determination to hold to the values he has come by so painfully since he has been in England. Daphne, the girl whom he thinks he loves and who has been with him during most of his off-duty hours on the tour, has found out as directly and cruelly as possible Buzz Marrow's terrible secret. Not only this secret, but the way in which Daphne has made Marrow confess, have pushed Boman to the limits of his self-control.

At this point, the morning of the raid, he has hated Marrow for three days; and, in hating him, he has been led to a bleak view of life generally. "War equalled s—— and peace equalled s——," he muses alone in the latrine. He had lost "the other Marrow," and perhaps he had lost his other self in the bargain. And because she had brought him the news, he thinks that he has lost the person who has now become "the other Daphne." Everything is contributing to the making of a disastrous mission, and Boman is almost past the point of caring about it. The novel, then, heads toward the eventual disclosure of what Daphne learned about Marrow, the recovery in the progress of the raid of a love for life which Boman had gained through loving Daphne, and the violent resolution of a matter of life and death at the end of this fated twenty-fourth mission.

The Body takes off in the grey early morning of hatred and foreboding, and the narrative returns to the earlier Marrow and Boman upon their arrival in England. The difference between the two men is apparent from their reactions to having flown the Atlantic. Boman notes: "As we eased down out of some low clouds the color of soft-coal smoke and saw England, after the strain, boredom, and cold of those many hours over the ocean, it was not the haycocks and hedgerows and heydownderry that attracted my eyes, but rather the black streaks at the end of a long concrete runway where rubber had burned from the wheels of other men's ships as they touched back to earth" (48).

Marrow, on the other hand, never seems to reflect consciously upon survival. He puts the ship down in a gentle landing because he is "a flying genius" and then bellows the first of a stream of joyful obscenities. He is apparently all vitality, strength, and bravado; impenetrably egotistical, he still commands the worshipful attention of the whole crew. The relationship is specific and ironic: Boman, the navigator, the bombardier, and the enlisted men all have absolute confidence in Marrow's ability to bring them through the tour alive. Everything obnoxious about the man seems to steel their one common conviction about his value.

Without having the charm dispelled, Boman, however, begins to make many strange observations about Marrow. The man is a habitually boastful lecher, but his sincerest boast comes when he talks about the first time he saw an airplane: "Just seeing that thing makes me feel horny." Claiming a little later to have made love to three nurses while in flight, Marrow says: "Flying's as good as getting it, and when you do it, too, bang, bang." And Marrow rarely talks about the war. "Why don't those frogs go jump in the lake?" he grunts, upon learning that the French radio had complained about a gross error in a raid on Rennes that had killed three hundred civilians. Boman reflects: "To Marrow war was a simple matter. It concerned his potency, his destructiveness. That there might be human beings with him or against him scarcely entered his head" (72). And this attitude seems proven after an abortive fight in a London bar, when Marrow sobs, "I'd like to kill 'em all."

While Boman never identifies with Marrow, even in the early days when he believes in the pilot as a talisman of survival, he proceeds very slowly to discover just how fully and in how many ways he differs from him. One such intimation comes to him after his London leave when he goes cycling with the unit meteorologist on a day when the sky overhead is a brilliant blue. Boman recognizes how much he has in common with the earth-bound weatherman as they talk about the legendary flight of Icarus and turn to the question of man's primitive curiosity. He realizes that such topics would never occur to his vaunted pilot. The meteorologist was ". . . content to imagine the Blanchard balloon with its curious feather-like oars, drifting across the

English Channel. With Buzz it had to be speed, daring, records, accidents, death, self. For Marrow the vault of heaven was only a mirror . . ." (77-78).

Boman is with Marrow when he first sees Daphne. Seeing her at the bar, Boman suppresses his reaction hoping that the great lecher may somehow miss her. Marrow does see her seconds later and commandeers her for their table; but the great surprise of this first encounter for Boman is that the girl pointedly prefers him to the pilot, and makes Marrow accept her preference. Hersey might be accused of romantic contrivance here, except for the care he has taken with the circumstances. Daphne has become a "dead man's drag"; she has arrived at the party on the base without having been told that her date has failed to return from the day's mission. Her mourning is perfunctory, but not indecently so: ". . . She was in love—not with poor Pitt any more, but with everyone, herself, life. She poured out warmth to a lot of men who were chilled to the bone. I had the illusion, however—and whether or not I was justified, I clung to it, a lamppost in my reeling world—that the only person to whom she communicated real feeling was me" (92).

Daphne becomes real enough in the course of the story, but she has a charismatic quality that goes beyond routine specifications for a serviceman's wartime romance. Once they meet, she possesses Boman entirely; and, gaining her, he possesses all that surrounds him when they are together. England becomes more than an air base and a few "liberty" towns: "I had come to have vivid, powerful feelings about all that damp green plate of landscape, seen in many lights. It had meant, so often, departure toward danger and then arrival back to safety; parting from Daphne, perhaps for the last time and then the prospect of reunion, relieved and weary, glad to be alive for her sake" (95). Daphne becomes the center of a mystique of living which includes rooms in which they have stayed, the English towns and rivers and countryside, the Tate Gallery and the Cambridge madrigal singers, and the renewed memories of the England of Boman's boyhood reading. But neither she nor England is purely a sentimental attachment; *The War Lover* is far from being such a paean of transatlantic ties as *The White Cliffs of Dover*.

To Boman, whose duty leaves him little to imagine but death or survival until the next mission, Daphne offers the challenge and complexity of living. She cannot be taken for granted, loyal and loving as she may be. As he comes to know her, Boman recognizes the truth of his first observation that she was in love with herself, with everybody, with life. It comes to him in such responses to her company as on one occasion after they had spent long hours talking about themselves. Boman recalls a mackerel sky that he had seen as a boy back in New England, while Daphne talks about a summer-house in her family's garden and her brother's model railway. Neither really listens to the other, but Boman suddenly understands something about the nature of love that had escaped him with all other women he had known before:

> . . . I was not listening to her too carefully, for I was thinking of what I could tell her next to impress her with my sensitivity, my kindness, my warmth, the ideality of my parents, my high regard for everything. Daphne was trying to impress me in the same way, I guess, and probably she was not really listening to me, either. But strangely enough, each of us, so concerned with our own excellent qualities, came through that conversation to appreciate each other more than before, even though he took in little of what was said.
>
> This feeling of self-love, the first step toward the love of someone else, was a source of inner strength for me, and I wanted to let Daphne know that ever since I had been in this room with her the last time, I had felt stronger, more sufficient to my tasks. (136)

At the height of his self-assurance in the relationship with Daphne, he brings Marrow along for lunch and listens to the story of his life. It is a blunt, vulgar, self-betraying account of the women he has taken to bed, the planes he has flown, and the cars he has owned. "But what about the war?" Daphne asks him. "Never had it so good," he exclaims. "I like to fly. I like the work we're doing . . . Boman here and I belong to the most destructive group of men in the history of the world" (144). This statement is too blunt, of course; Marrow sounds far more convincing when he lies about his sexual conquests than when he speaks truly about his love of bombing. Here it becomes apparent that this novel is really about the life lover, rather than the war lover, and that Marrow is given such speeches for the purpose of showing the reader how sensitive Boman has become by contrast, and, for the sake of the story, to further the contest between Marrow and Daphne over Boman's soul. Daphne is

alerted at this meeting to the necessity which drives her to con-
front Marrow in her bedroom before the twenty-fourth mission
and goad him into a suicidal awareness of what he really is.

As in most war novels, there are several minor figures just
sufficiently identified as individuals in a military organization
to provide a realistic environment for the major characters. The
most interesting minor figure in *The War Lover* is Kid Lynch,
another co-pilot, who has been killed in action shortly before
Boman's twenty-fourth mission. His contribution to Boman's
enlightenment is not entirely clear. He is somewhat like Boman
in being sensitive to war aims and the philosophical implications
of survival; but, as a minor character, he is given the fairly common fictional role of the eccentric intellectual. At his best, he is
an Irish poet who grabs the base's public address systems on one
despairing evening to recite from one of his peers:

> Now hear this. . . . Footnote on morale!
> Those that I fight I do not hate
> Those that I guard I do not love . . .
> Nor law, nor duty bade my fight,
> Nor public men, nor cheering crowds.
> A lonely impulse of delight
> Drove to this tumult in the clouds.[4]

And he entertains a credulous Marrow with the legend of a
Black Knight of the Luftwaffe who drinks a vial of captured
flyers' blood before each mission. The poetic Lynch, in his
allusive way, understands Marrow in much the same way that
Daphne later reveals him to Boman. Lynch predicts that Boman
will survive Marrow because he has the imagination that the
pilot lacks: "To imagine *is* to suffer. Really, it's very painful, but
you get used to it. The man without imagination takes a lot, he
doesn't even bat an eyelash. But when he does break, goodbye!
He's gone and you can't salvage him" (230).

Lynch's professed war aim complements Yeats's poem: "If I
can do my part in keeping this worst side of mankind in hand,
I'll be satisfied, whatever happens to me." He is killed by straf-
ing bullets that spatter his brain against the bulkhead of his
crippled plane. When Boman meets the plane as it bumps to a
halt on the field and helps to remove Lynch's body, he feels responsible for his friend's death because he had not warned the
unit of Lynch's extreme anxiety over a letter from his faithless
wife. The next day Daphne shocks Boman by leading him to

understand how this feeling actually masked a hatred of Lynch because of the poet's superior awareness of what the war and living and Marrow are all about. Once Boman understands, he is able to mourn Lynch genuinely, free of self-pity. Only at that point, actually, does he begin to prepare for the twenty-fourth mission and the fulfillment of Lynch's prophecy.

With this instance of Boman's increasing association of Daphne with all that life will ever hold for him, the novel returns to the raid to keep pace with the changing nature of the complex relationships of the crew aboard *The Body*. Marrow has acted strangely since the moment of the take-off. Encountering enemy fighters at the European coast, he now flies to keep himself alive instead of trying to uncover as many of the plane's guns as possible to the enemy. He misses almost every chance of shooting down German fighters, bewildering and angering the crew. He is silent when he would ordinarily curse his crewmen over the intercom and then vindictive in a whining monotone until no one pays any attention to him. Throughout the flight, his face and his eyes take on strangely fixed expressions.

Routine requests from the crewmen now come directly to Boman, who acknowledges them without nodding to the pilot and then wonders for a vagrant second at the change in command. When a bullet hits the third engine, Boman, without hesitating, acknowledges the tail gunner's report and orders the silent Marrow to kill the fuel to the third engine. Next Marrow is by-passed on another crewman's question about the emergency, and Boman takes a moment to reflect on the fact that he is now running the ship. Marrow continues the actions of flying the ship, his manipulative reactions still sure; but now he seems to be completely indifferent to the results of the mission. When *The Body* takes a sharp hit in the nose and starts falling, Marrow's "miraculous reflex" pulls it out of an incipient spin, but from then on he is finished as anything but an automatic pilot.

Boman becomes fully responsible for holding the plane's altitude until it can clear the enemy coast on its return home, as well as for every other decision that could come before a commanding officer in a flight toward life or death. When Marrow reaches the stage in his collapse where he is no longer even able to manipulate the controls sensibly, Boman gestures him to the co-pilot's seat and takes over the last aspect of command.

With Boman at the controls, the story flashes back a last time to the tour and to the disclosure of what went on in Daphne's room during Marrow's visit. The pilot had arrived uninvited with his Distinguished Flying Cross in one hand and a fifth of whiskey in the other. (The medal had been awarded him a few days before with his promotion to major.) He had begun by vaguely belittling Boman as not "real gutsy . . . too educated or something." Then he turned to his abiding themes of speed and fighting, the cars he had owned, and his mad money—two fifty-dollar bills, which he suddenly pulled from his wallet and thrust on Daphne's bed. Then, to Boman's complete devastation as he is told the story, Daphne went to bed with the pilot. Hersey sacrifices credibility and some of the illusions that he has carefully nurtured about the relationship between Boman and Daphne in order to explain the auto-erotic basis of Buzz Marrow's behavior, a risky decision hastily covered by the claim that Daphne has done this also because she doubts the steadiness of Boman's love. At any rate, Boman's new understanding of his pilot is bought at a hard price.

When she told Boman these things, Daphne insisted that Marrow did not "really" make love to her because he was incapable of doing so. He was exactly like an earlier R.A.F. war lover to whom she had given herself, a man who "wanted to use [her] to make love to himself." Her unresponsiveness had driven Marrow into an abusive torrent of recrimniation past any sensibility of the actual situation. He admitted that the slighted Boman was actually capable and courageous; that the Distinguished Flying Cross was undeserved; but, that under no circumstances should Daphne think that he, Marrow, was cowardly: "I'll, I'll bomb the bejeezus. . . . Don't make the mistake he [Boman] did. Don't you get it into your head that the reason I didn't want to go around the second time was because I was chicken s---. Oh no, baby. The only reason was, I didn't care where the f--- we dropped those bombs, as long as it was on a city. You can't win a war being squeamish. Chicken s--- doesn't win wars. You have to kill *somebody*" (381).

At this precise moment, Daphne tells him that she knows all about him. She knows all about the feeling he has—that "stirring down there" when he starts his bombing run. His "gratification wells up out of the dark slimy place of toads and snakes and hairy men." He is a war lover in the most literal, sordid sense of the word. The abstraction pursued throughout the novel is fleshed out, and brutal sense is made of what Sherman and Patton had said before Marrow had been created to exemplify what they meant.

A question remains for Boman (as it had for any reader concerned with the probability of Daphne's complaisance, however intellectually motivated), and the girl's answer is not at all comforting. She had also gone to bed with Marrow because life goes on and because Boman's tour was nearly over; and, as it drew to a close, Daphne had come to feel that Boman had not wanted her much more than Marrow had—differently, of course, but not much more. She compelled him to consider just what he had meant by "selfless love," or if his commitment to their mutual happiness was much different from the shaky compromise he had worked out for himself on bombing missions: he would go along with the flight, but was determined not to kill anyone. Boman leaves the apartment heartsick and confused over Daphne, but he is armed with all that he needs to know about his pilot. The story then moves swiftly to its conclusion with the end of the raid.

A stupefied Marrow is trussed up in the radio shack, orders and compliances go back and forth from Boman to the crew, and all prepare for the shock of hitting the water. Boman considers Marrow for the last time:

> Not only had he been free of fear in combat; he had enjoyed our missions, he had enjoyed them too much, and it may be that he had come at the end to fear not the clashes and killing but his enjoyment of them. For to enjoy, even to enjoy horror, was to live, AND much as he had shouted about his zest for life, I believe Buzz had found life, at the innermost heart of it, unbearable. . . . *The Body,* his body as he imagined had been opened up to let death in. He was maimed. His power and manliness were not untouchable at all; they were being taken away from him. Because of the inner drive for death he did not know he had, he passively welcomed his emasculation and disarmament. Now he was hurrying home. . . . Marrow had begun to mimic, with heartbreaking authority, a final approach to the death he unknowingly wanted. (396)

There is Boman's last mention of Daphne, a Daphne fused with all of England, that may be a happy portent:

> I loved England. I wanted England. Dimly in the distance to the left I could see the tall bluffs of the east coast, the stretch, the stretch from Dover to Margate, where the glare path of the sun

ended in shadow. I was straining every nerve and muscle to get as far as I could. . . . I wanted a miracle to buoy me to England . . . I wanted Daphne. I wanted, just once more, to be with my Daph, to lie on my back in a meadow by a sluggish stream, with my head in her lap, talking about us. Couldn't I see her once more, to tell her I'd meant to handle things differently? I wanted another chance at life. Couldn't a man try again, and get it right this time? (399)

The Body crash lands, submerges, and splits in two, then briefly rights itself in the water. All the crew are able to get out, but as they prepare to pull away, Boman notices Marrow bobbing against the fuselage. He swims up to him, tugs at him, and is pushed away. The pilot turns frantically to his sinking plane, and clutches a propeller blade which takes him down. And then "We were all on the rescue boat soon, and with a roar it lifted its head and raced toward England. I looked back. There was a broad wake of churning spindrift, almost like a contrail in the sky. Except for that path the sea was barren. There was not a trace of Marrow, who had loved war, or of his ship, which he had named *The Body*" (404).

The end of war must mean a return to living, and those who loved war must die with it. Boman and Daphne may find a way of making a life together for each has shown some aspiration for meaningful survival. Daphne may have taught Boman how to love and, along the way, herself. Whatever they have become and whatever they will do overshadows at the close of the novel the very explicit thing that Buzz Marrow has become.

Hersey might have written a much simpler novel about the erotic motivation of warriors. Marrow's final act might have taken all hands down with *The Body,* save for Boman's bailing out or being thrown loose like Ishmael. However, the story became more complicated, more interesting, if, at times, vaguer in its implications. *A War Lover* marks still further distance from the reporter to the novelist—the reporter who could deliver neatly fictionalized theses in *A Bell for Adano* and the novelist who found himself dealing with the ambiguities of war. The logic of his career compelled Hersey to write about life-lovers whose motives and actions are much more difficult to know than the psychic contrail of war-lover Buzz Marrow.

CHAPTER 6

The Child Buyer

H ERSEY'S long-standing interest in educational problems led
him to write *The Child Buyer* (1960). The book effectively denounces the abuse of intelligence in American education
and often flares into a satire of American purposes and institutions beyond the classroom. A powerful, awkward novel, some of
its limitations are suggested by the description on the title page:
"A Novel in the Form of Hearings before the Standing Committee on Education, Welfare, & Public Morality of a certain
State Senate, Investigating the conspiracy of Mr. Wissey Jones,
with others, to Purchase a Male Child."

Everything that Hersey wishes to say on the subject of education and everything that a reader may learn about a complicated
plot with numerous characters is packed into the form of com-
mittee-hearing transcriptions. It is too great a burden, however
vividly "point of order! point of order!" may yet echo with
readers who followed the McCarthy hearing telecasts of the
mid-1950's. The "conspiracy" itself is difficult to accept, even as
a satirist's proposal; for Hersey submits that Americans are so
incapable of dealing with genius and so overawed by any appeal in the name of "national security" that any one of them
could reach a point where he would justify selling the "male
child," Barry Rudd, to United Lymphomilloid for the purpose
of converting him into a superbeing, a human computer with
all his senses "tied off" so that he may achieve an IQ reaching
toward 1000.

But *The Child Buyer* represents a carefully considered decision as to form and content, reached after several years of study
and hard work. The list of Hersey's activities in education[1] is as
extensive as the records of political commitment by novelists of
the 1920's and 1930's who spent so much of their time on picket
lines and lent their names to letterheads. Between 1950 and
1952, Hersey was a member of the Westport, Connecticut,
Board of Education, concerned with budgets, hiring and firing,

building specifications, as well as with curricula and methods. Between 1954 and 1958 he was a consultant for the Fund for the Advancement of Education; in 1955, he was a delegate to the White House Conference on Education. He expressed his own opinions, listened to others, and went on record with the consensus statements of these large groups. Most recently he has been a member of the Weston, Connecticut, Board of Education. Short of actually teaching or becoming an administrator, he has run the gamut of responsibility in the field. From all of these experiences, Hersey gained particular knowledge about such matters as educational testing, guidance, "enrichment," and teaching methods, all of which are effectively attacked in *The Child Buyer*.

His most pressing interest in education, however, has been the care and development of the bright student, especially the one who may become lost in the machinery of democratic education. Hersey's own schooling, it should be noted, was generally of a sort where bright children would be noticed: the small classes for English and American children in China, the small public schools of Briarcliff Manor, Hotchkiss, Yale, and Clare College. Neither he nor anyone he knew throughout his formal education could possibly have qualified as a neglected prodigy.

His first writing on anyone remotely like this was a by-product of his wartime reporting, "The Brilliant Jughead," a *New Yorker* article about an enlisted man who had gone through the United States Army school for illiterates in Harrisburg, Pennsylvania.[2] Hersey reported how the army had been able to give this man and thirteen thousand others the equivalent of a sixth-grade education in three months of intensive training. Reading was integrated with writing in a course that carefully recognized the problems of the adult illiterate by taking up adult subjects and consistently appealing to the individual's pride.

This experience offered a comforting paradox that Hersey remembered when studying the education of children in the public schools: the traditionally impersonal United States Army had taken great pains to recognize the merits of each soldier-illiterate. Classes never dragged as civilian instructors balanced their presentations skillfully between informal conversation and exacting drill. Hersey was especially struck by the appreciation shown by graduates of this program. His own subject had reacted to this opportunity with feeling: They can take away my gun, also my uniform, but they won't ever take away how to read and write.

In a report on reading problems in *Life* nine years later,[3] Hersey attacked the "distortion of the philosophical assumption of 'teaching the whole child.'" First of thirty-six objectives in reading readiness, according to one teacher's manual on the pre-primer level, was "feeling of pleasure"; twenty-first was "to develop ability to read short sentences." The cult of wholeness had brought about such vague terms as "language arts" to replace "reading and writing"; and the accompanying cult of uniformity led to much worse effects upon the students. Overworked teachers too often encouraged mediocrity by failing to push brighter students into more difficult material; instead they offered them "enrichment"—in many cases merely a break from routine to such time-passing occupations as straightening out filing systems or correcting spelling papers.

The writing which precisely foreshadowed *The Child Buyer* was a twenty-eight-page pamphlet, published by the Woodrow Wilson Foundation in 1959, "Intelligence, Choice, and Consent." In it Hersey describes the plight of a twelve-year-old girl from a lower income family, who is victimized by having had her high verbal ability overlooked by careless testing, by ignorant school officials, and most of all by a false concept of egalitarianism in American public education. The essay was written against the immediate background of "crash programs" throughout the public school system in response to the post-Sputnik urgency on behalf of national defense, and at the end of a period of historical progression from education as a privilege for the few to an education accessible to all. Hersey's was a difficult position for a liberal and a humanitarian to assert, but he was determined to show that the noblest democratic intentions are no guarantee of excellence in education.

According to Hersey, the very fact that this nation recoiled from any thought of an educated aristocracy led to a distortion of the opposing tendency. Teaching was leveled for and to the mythical average student. Ideals were scaled down to norms; and the IQ tests, which had begun through the careful experimentation of Binet and Terman, developed oversimplified offshoots administrable by anyone interested in screening talent. They even gave Professor William Bagley of Columbia Teachers' College a range of 85 to 115 for his definition of the common man, the preferred beneficiary of American schooling. The nation developed schools in which Hersey's twelve-year-old-girl became lost and from which one could scarcely hope to find the special intelligence needed to sustain American democracy in a world in which most nations directed their educational programs toward their most intelligent students. Hersey wrote:

> . . . The work of the Manhattan Project in developing the atomic bomb seems to have convinced many people that all that is needed to unlock supreme mysteries, such as cancer or talent, is an act of Congress, or the banding together of many vast agencies, and expenditures of huge sums of money. But the job of freeing talent does not lend itself to this kind of attack. Ability is elusive; genius wilts in a bureaucratic setting. Intelligence of a high order is mysterious, manifold, fast-moving, luminous, tantalizing, and incredibly beautiful. . . . (12)

And such intelligence may be found among those who are termed "common men." Hersey effectively counters the democratic bias against exceptional intelligence in backgrounds of modest means and by suggesting in his notations on the deprivations of Janet Train and her once-bright mother that a sympathetic environment makes a great difference. Intelligence may be correlated with vitality, and both may be fluid and variable and dependent upon the emotional life of the individual in whom they are found.

If these facts could be recognized, Hersey argues, the nation might approach a true equality of opportunity to replace the overly simple notion to which it had been clinging. But this possibility, as Janet Train's school and town made all too plain, was being halted in school after school throughout the United States. Too many school authorities met the issue the way the superintendent of schools in Janet's home town did: "I'm afraid of anything too special for these clever children. I'm afraid of it for our city. We don't like anything that smacks of privilege. But don't worry, we reach those children. We'll reach them with enrichment" (23). So Janet, put to work at a filing system to become enriched, went home after school to read her older sister's movie magazines.

Truly democratic education, Hersey argues, depends on the schools being ready for the unexpected: the intelligence which isn't instantly measurable or instantly summoned by a national crisis. The anger which could conceive of United Lymphomilloid in *The Child Buyer* is only a little subdued in the final passage of the pamphlet:

> . . . The failure here is a failure of national vision—for we have tended to see human beings as statistics, children as weapons, talents as materials capable of being mined, assayed, and fabricated for profit and defense. We have the cart before the horse if we think that we can order up units of talent for the national defense. The only sure defense of democracy will be its inner growth, and the first essential of this growth is something far less grandiose but far more difficult to realization than a National Defense Education Act, or a crash program under any other title—namely, a true recognition that each child in each classroom in our schools is a unique human being, who one day must make choices and give consents that will help to perfect us all. (27-28)

This modestly circulated pamphlet went far beyond any of the writer's more widely published statements on education in national magazines.[4] Indeed, it offered the basic ideas to be terrifyingly developed in *The Child Buyer*: the supreme value of individual intelligence and the tragic inability of present-day American society to cope with it.

The Child Buyer extends this lucid exposition into a sustained irony. Barry Rudd, the bright child, becomes a prodigy in the novel, not simply a slum child with an IQ of between 130 and 144, as in Janet Train's case; he has literally one mind in a million. At the age of nine, his greatest pleasure is to "tell you the family, genus, species, and subspecies of every bird—every living thing you could imagine. In Latin." Teachers and other school officials are made into caricatures of the uncritical egalitarians mentioned in the pamphlet. The guidance expert boasts of a test "that gives the equivalent of three years of psychoanalysis in twenty minutes." The district superintendent is incapable of making a coherent statement because of all the professional jargon that clutters his talk.

The misuse of intelligence, once stated simply as seeing "human beings as statistics, children as weapons," becomes the monstrous project for which the child buyer, Wissey Jones, is an advance agent. This self-possessed, conniving individual reveals the plan in a closed session of the committee near the end of the hearings. The bright children purchased by U Lympho are sealed in dark, barren cells, six feet square, for a period of several weeks; they see and hear nothing except piped-in whisperings of the goodness of U Lympho—"the motherly, protective, nourishing qualities of the corporate image, and later to Her creativity, fecundity, and later still to her Great Mystery—the Miracle of the Fifty-Year Project." And, all the while, the victim is being fed dosages of the drug "L. T." (*lethe terrae*) to induce forgetfulness of all earthly things. This period is followed by one of "education and desensitization in isolation" during which the subject is put into a small room with no windows, never again to "look out at the complexity of nature, which would only confuse him." His re-education proceeds from toilet-training through higher mathematics on tape and an array of television and radio programs especially prepared for him to accept U Lympho as Truth and the Source and Secret of Life. The subject's "whole life becomes an attempt to please Her by spurts of creative mental activity, which are seen as worshipful acts." Then, the subject is transferred to a three-week data-feeding process by calculating machines which, in turn, have been fed by previously conditioned specimens. The horror becomes concrete:

> The subject is now perfectly prepared to do Her work. There are, however, two dangers. One is that through some inadvertence, unforeseen by the minds of the technicians who have not been conditioned as the specimen has, scraps of information that are not wholly related to the subject's particular area of worship-solving may creep into his mind. The second is that he may develop emotions: it has been found that, despite the prophylaxis and enthohexylcenteron, extremely dangerous emotions may arise, apparently stemming from tiny doubts about Her, the source of which Project researchers have not yet been able to pin down. The specimen therefore undergoes major surgery, which consists of "tying off" all five senses. Since the subject need not take in any more data, he has no further need of sight and hearing. Smell and taste have long since been useless to him, since he regards the intake of food as a mechanical process that he carries on only for Her sake. Only so much sense of touch is left the specimen as to allow him to carry on his bodily functions and "write" on a simplomat recorder, a stenographic machine the use of which has long since become a ceremonial rite for the subject. Most subjects are also sterilized, though a certain few will be left their reproductive equipment in order to breed further specimens for the Project. (207-8)

"Productive work" is the final stage. "The specimen worships U Lympho by offering up to Her solutions of incredibly difficult problems relating to the Mystery." The Mystery itself is unknown even to the Child Buyer, who believes, however, that it has to do with satisfying "man's greatest need—to leave the earth." How, one senator asks, can *this* relate to national defense? The answer is simple. U Lympho has a government defense contract; and, if one wishes to become philosophical about the project, "in the present state of affairs the best defense might be departure."

One would suppose that even the moronic Senator Voyolko of the investigating committee would recognize that such a Mystery would be diametrically opposed to any objectives for the education of human beings, yet the suspense of the novel lies not so much in the eventual disclosure of U Lympho but in reaching the several points at which each character, even Barry Rudd himself, acquiesces to the sale. "Everyone who has the slightest hold on a child . . . asks—and usually gets—a price," Wissey Jones says of his operation at his first committee appearance. Indeed, everyone is paid off except Mr. Owings, the district superintendent, who is too wound up in his own rhetoric to listen to the proposition.

The guidance man, Mr. Cleary, is easily won by the offer of an assistant superintendent's position under an aging superior in a wealthy district. Cleary had picked guidance as his field because it offered short-cuts to position and security that no teaching position could ever match. Tests are the stuff of Cleary's life. With the Foundation for National Superiority in Education paying the bills, he led a "talent search" in Pequot by testing for intellectual gifts, creativity, leadership, aggressive maladjustment, and potential alcoholism. He is particularly fond of the Olmstead-Diffendorff Game, an "improvement" on the verbally-loaded Stanford-Binet tests because it consists "entirely of problems developed by cartoons in comic-book style, and drawing heavily for content on the child's world of television, sports, toys, and gadgets, [it] is culture-free and without social bias." Despite his dislike of Barry Rudd, Cleary knows that the boy has passed the only tests that could interest the child buyer, and he has no trouble overcoming his own democratic biases when he is offered a sure chance for power.

Barry's teachers are more formidable obstacles. Miss Charity

Perrin is a sixty-year-old spinster who lives only for loving her pupils and being loved by them. Although not an inspiring teacher, she is a tolerant person just fond enough of individual intelligence to resist the findings of an Olmstead-Diffendorff Game. Once, in her youth, she was not the gentle, passive woman who trembles before the committee; and that was when the Depression had forced her into a picket line during an abortive teachers' strike. Committee counsel Broadbent and its reactionary member, Senator Skypack, seize upon this information for much more than it is worth in the course of the hearings, but it becomes the basis of Miss Perrin's eventual sellout. The child buyer offers her a flat sum which will enable her to retire to immunity from any possible persecution as a "Red."

Miss Frederika Gozar, on the other hand, seems thoroughly invulnerable. She is a paragon of hard-boiled virtues, incredibly learned and disciplined for an elementary school principal. Miss Gozar holds four master's degrees and one doctorate; sleeps only four hours a night so that she can work another four hours in a biology laboratory before going to her desk in the morning; judges at track meets only because she has become too old to compete; knows almost everything that Barry Rudd knows; and, of course, runs her school with exemplary efficiency in a running battle with the guidance man, the district superintendent, state officials, and the Parent Teachers Association.

Beyond these accomplishments, Dr. Gozar articulates everything that Hersey himself had ever said about intelligence. "I believe in the infinite potentiality of young people," she testifies; "and I think I can do something about it." A crash program for intelligence is the worst possible way of approaching the commodity: "We'll be having a crash program to locate God one of these days, pin down a definite location for His throne" (64-65). Dr. Gozar, almost as much as Barry himself, is U Lympho's obvious antagonist and the most eminently qualified heroine for this terrible struggle; and so she seems for most of the novel. After all, she was the person who discovered Barry Rudd, permitted him to work with her in the lab, constantly pushed aside all limits on his curiosity. If Barry really wants to understand the reproductive process of mammals, Dr. Gozar guides him to the necessary books and is thoroughly sympathetic when he plays "doctor" with a girl classmate to discredit himself with the Child Buyer.

When this little encounter becomes a town scandal and the subject of a parents' meeting to hear an "enrichment" expert, Dr. Gozar makes a hugely successful stink bomb to disrupt the proceedings. She seems completely without personal vanity and one impossible to counter by niceties or conventional logic. "This is a man's world, and I've gotten used to talking like a man to make my way in it," she boasts. She is won over finally, and not very credibly, by an appeal to her intellectual vanity. Barry, she believes, can defy U Lympho, going through the project without forgetting the earth to which he was born:

> Talent is a hundred times as fragile as crystal from Venice. It can't stand up under hammer blows of stupidity—least of all, those of stupid notoriety. Barry's finished as far as the world of Pequot and Treehampstead and what he has called home is concerned. Thanks to you gentlemen. So that the chance of something remarkable being salvaged at United Lymphomilloid seems to me worth taking. And if he fails, if he does forget, and if they do turn him into a machine, he'll be the best; he (or it) will have an IQ of twelve hundred, fifteen hundred. How the wheels will turn! (250-51)

When she is made to realize that Wissey Jones has been after her approval at any price, whether Barry is sent with her orders to defy or comply, she retires abjectly.

Barry Rudd's parents are almost exact counterparts of Janet Train's. His mother has a useless faculty of total recall, has been a voracious reader whose tastes have deteriorated from Victorian novels to movie magazines, keeps a slovenly household, and prizes her son's talents as the only token of her own fading pretensions of gentility. The boy's father is a machinist who began to work for a living when he was Barry's age. The child buyer's offer strikes him as his just reward for rearing a strange, unrewarding child. Mrs. Rudd battles away for most of the novel, adhering to her own notions of mother love. Her breaking point is reached brutally when the child buyer stages a hoodlum attack on the tenement where the family lives. In her anger, Mrs. Rudd begins shouting obscenities in front of her children and instantly destroys the image of herself and, so she believes, the maternal dignity by which she had secured her children. In stating the terms of her sellout, Hersey indulges a few satiric comments on American culture outside the public school system:

Thanks to Mr. Jones, we'll be surrounded by the best works of man. I mean, he's going to give us the Five-Foot-Three-Inch Classics Shelf, in de-luxe imitation-leather bindings, and a subscription to the Upstream Book Society, where every month you can practically read right over the shoulders of Aubrey Winston, Pierre Berlioz, and Willing Lion, the judges . . . and the Sky-Hi-Fi Symphony Series, complete in sixty albums, and a composite stereophonic record player, and the Print of the Month, matted and framed, from the Modenheim Museum, and the *Drawn and Quartered Quarterly*, the digest of all the biggest Little Magazines . . . and a new television—I'm not ashamed of this, it's part of our American culture—so we can view The Endless Mind, and Shortcuts to Longhair Music, and The United States Motor Company Shakespeare Half Hour. And a cleaning woman once a week. All the cultural opportunities I've ever dreamed of. (245)

Mr. Rudd is content with such a quiz-show prize as a red sports car.

The final party to the agreement is the child himself, and his eventual reasons for deciding to leave Pequot for U Lympho are extremely convincing when compared to the motives attributed to the people who sell him. Barry Rudd's IQ is 189 (Stanford-Binet, tested at age five—approximately the IQ of Bentham, Leibnitz, Macaulay, and Grotius, and higher than those of Voltaire, Descartes, Darwin, Newton, and Lope de Vega.) It is masked by a pale, impassive face set upon a fat, slow-moving body. The shrewd observer, Wissey Jones, describes him further: ". . . when words that stand for strong feelings pass the short, tight lips, only a flicker of expression, like distant heat lightning, can be seen around the eyes, which are startlingly clear, direct, and alert." According to Dr. Gozar, the boy is characterized by curiosity and intensity, neither of which shows on the surface.

No description could prepare the reader for the range and quality of Barry's testimony. His first utterance is not the required response to the witness's oath, but an admission that he is a skeptic. Then, we see the randomness of his curiosity:

Miss Henley [the state office "enrichment" authority] reminds me of the word "bipinnatifid." I'm not sure exactly why, unless it's that Miss Henley uses the first-personal singular pronoun so much, and there are four i's in bipinnatifid. By the way, do you know a common eight-letter word, we all use it every day, with only one vowel in it? . . . It's an easy word. Anyway, to get back to "bipinnatifid." When I was in second grade, I saw a brown thrasher for the first time, *Toxostoma rufum*, and heard it sing its mocking song, like a mockingbird's, only funnier, truly humorous, and I didn't know what it was, so I described it to Miss Songevine, my teacher at that time, and she showed me the color plate, Common Birds of America, in the big Webster, and I remember that "bipinnatifid" was at the top of the opposing page, and I looked up its meaning, and that got me interested in leaves and their comparative forms. . . . (74-75)

Clearly, Hersey would have difficulty presenting even a randomly inclined junior Linnaeus without making him seem a U Lympho specimen already run through the process; so there is a sudden, precocious touch of the poet as the boy describes a walk through the woods:

. . . I only know I'll never be as happy again as I was the other afternoon in the woods. The white oaks made a kind of backdrop, because, you know, they hold their leaves the longest, like small leather gloves, still solid green; while the elms and hickories had gone brown early in the dry August we had this year, and in the wind on Ella's [the hurricane] train the week before they'd been almost stripped, and their skeletons made a blackish mesh, so the displays of the other trees seemed even more prodigal: deep coppers of the sumac and dogwood, pure yellows of the birches, and, here and there, ironwood and sassafras, and, best of all, the incredible orange glow of hard maples—like the inside of a Halloween pumpkin when the candle's lit. . . . (77)

He loves words: "Oh, yes! Kismet, hieratic, mellific, nuncupative, sempiternal, mansuetude, peremiad, austral, diaphanous, hegemony. . ." Yet he strains one's belief most by seeming, in his testimony, to know himself even more thoroughly than he knows the classification of living things. He does not think that he's a genius, except in the sense that he would like to work as hard as he can. He knows precisely how clumsy he is at games, how childishly he may respond to his young sister's teasing, and how callously he may behave toward his parents. He is more accurate in appraising his talents than Miss Gozar is: "I'm not maladjusted. I'm intensified."

While his parents haggle over him, Barry tries his own devices to discourage the child buyer. A delinquent classmate shrewdly advises him to get into trouble of some kind as the best means to incur adult disfavor. Hence, he stages the "doctor game" with his complaisant little classmate in such an awkward fashion as to insure being caught. Of course, had the disposition of his case been solely in the hands of school authorities, he would have been entirely successful and won the notoriety that the committee counsel and at least one of the senators are eager to fasten on him. The child buyer is merely amused.

Barry is on hand to watch a meeting between the child buyer and the guidance counselor, where, with some detachment, he witnesses the "G-man's" breaking point. Faintly, Hersey traces the boy's growing awareness of the child buyer's system in approaching all interested adults in Pequot, and how he becomes convinced that any further life for him in the town would be meaningless. He comes to feel so despite a clear understanding of the nature of the U Lympho experiment, but he—alone—has a compelling reason for going away with the child buyer. He has decided that life at U Lympho would *at least be interesting* (my italics). This phrase, at the close of the hearings, summons back all of the testimony on "enrichment," testing, social adjustment, misinformation, neglect of talent, and disparagement. Hersey has concentrated all his compassion for bright children in Barry's comment. It is a terrifying final indictment of mid-century American society, made all the more poignant as Barry goes on to say something that shows him to be a child for all of his brilliance: "If all the pictures went out, if I forgot everything, where would they go? Just out in the air? Into the sky? Back home around my bed, where my dreams stay?" (258).

Brilliantly and bitterly, Hersey thus leads the reader to wonder if Barry has made so tragic a choice. The public schools, Hersey suggests, are kindlier but more haphazard U Lymphos. They misinform the child, "enrich" him with petty chores, and establish his precocity as queerness. A democratic education as conceived by its extremist adherents would, according to Hersey, make each classroom a Forgetting Chamber for the bright child. The procedures he so scathingly describes are, in effect, a workable crash program for mediocrity. Little wonder that a Barry Rudd caught in such a system would choose anything that he hoped might be interesting.

The Child Buyer is a powerful statement of Hersey's indignation, if one is content to read it as such. By imagining the worst possible situation for illustrating his point, he convinces most readers that there are disastrous tendencies in American public education. He makes it quite clear, as well, that Americans have tragic notions of the society that this education is meant to produce. Yet, one must regret that Hersey chose to constrict his passionate argument—not to mention his story and his characters—within the rigid format of "a novel in the form of a hearing." It is very difficult to know his more complex characters, particularly Miss Gozar and Barry himself, merely through their speeches and the impressions of other witnesses. And all the witnesses must be understood, realistically, as they react to the limited, predictable stimulus of questions from the three senators and their counsel. Senator Voyolko is a moron who limits his contributions to such questions as the screen size of the Rudds' promised television set. Senator Skypack is a cartoon figure on the lookout for deviates, subversives, and assorted non-conformists. The committee counsel is out to make a name for himself. Senator Mansfied is ineffectually well-meaning. Much of a novel's development has to be inserted in the form of somewhat irrelevant testimony.

Finally, one may question Hersey's choice of a victim. What if Barry Rudd had been simply another bright child instead of the peer of Leibnitz and Macaulay? Intelligence, as Hersey observed in the pamphlet preceding the novel, is elusive and tantalizingly beautiful, qualities far more poignant in the thousands of bright students shunted off to "enrichment" than in the nonpareil genius, Barry Rudd. A more credible victim would have been someone like Janet Train. Robert Gorham Davis, contributing to a *New Republic* symposium on *The Child Buyer*,[5] puts the matter more harshly when he states that Hersey was unsuccessful, even if the reader was asked to consider "an imaginative encounter with unreal beings living in various kinds of rapport with the real world of nature."

The Child Buyer, however, is successful despite its flaws. Its success is ironically confirmed by some of the other criticism in the *New Republic* symposium. B. F. Skinner—the Harvard psychologist who invented the teaching machine, wrote *Walden II*, and experimented with the "baby box"—was certainly struck by the force of Hersey's distortions. The situation in *The Child Buyer*, Professor Skinner stated with unintended irony, was implausible, the work of someone who "has been trying to do something about education." His review bore this innocent title: "May We Have a Positive Contribution?" Dr. Carl Hansen, Superintendent of Schools in the District of Columbia, saw in this novel "satire, as it always is, at the sacrifice of balance." Hersey, according to Dr. Hansen, should have been aware of the fact that education, at the working level, "demands more good sense than most people think." "Is knowledge now becoming man's master?" Dr. Hansen concluded. Such "attacks" hardly needed to be offset by the praise of Margaret Halsey and William Jay Smith in the same pages.

CHAPTER 7

White Lotus

> Man's greatest hazard of violence
> is not flood or fire or hurricane
> or ice or earthquake or famine;
> it is his own capacity to act on
> the worst in his nature.
>
> —*Here To Stay*

JOHN HERSEY would have to write some kind of a book about the racial problems of the 1960's, not because race had become a desirable topic for any self-consciously serious writer, but because racial struggles are the most revealing contemporary test of his lifelong theme: man's will to survive in a peaceful world. He said as much in the foreword to *Here To Stay* (1963), a collection of his reporting on this theme: "I could not claim that the stories in this book cover the front of man's grip on life. The volume leaves out, to give but two examples of omissions, the indomitability of the Royal Air Force that saved Britain from Hitler, and the struggle of the Negro in the United States for a proper share in what is called, sometimes without irony, 'the American way'" (viii).

Of course, this statement also implies that Hersey's wide range of reporting assignments had never brought him close to the problems of American Negroes. Indeed, he had never reported any phase of the civil rights movement; and, in facing the question as a possible subject, he was in the position of most white writers outside the South. He had read and admired Ralph Ellison's *Invisible Man*, in which a Negro novelist wrote not merely an account of conditions but also an allegory on the subtleties of racial identity.[1] Hersey recognized that while he could never acquire the special knowledge of Ellison or James Baldwin, he could perhaps work from an abstract consideration comparable to the one which had been at least half of the basis for *Invisible Man.* The alternative would have been a quick return to reporting and a book which dealt with particulars: "The Negro Problem in America" in any of several fictional guises or as a straightforward personal odyssey of meetings, demonstrations, and interviews. Such literature is abundant and variously authoritative on an academic level; it is done and re-done on a journalistic level; or it is frankly sensational and contrived in a spate of such novels as Irving Wallace's *The Man.*

The frontier of this subject for white writers may have been reached (where it has not been surpassed by Faulkner's special awareness) in two remarkable books, John Howard Griffin's *Black Like Me* and Norman Mailer's *The White Negro.*[2] Griffin, a Texan, faced his assignment more directly than has any other white American writer, living or dead. Through a drug treatment he changed his pigmentation temporarily so that he might be taken for a Negro. After this transformation, he traveled through several Southern states as a black stranger to both whites and Negroes and was able to experience literally being denied service at a restaurant or lodging at a hotel, having to step aside for a white man on a sidewalk, and, more important than anything else, day-to-day life as a Negro transient within Southern Negro communities. On this level of experience, he came nearer than any other white American to understanding the situation of Ellison's unnamed narrator.

Mailer began more abstractly in his conception of *The White Negro,* as Hersey would later in beginning to write *White Lotus.* He defined the hipster as a white Negro by way of disproving anyone else's definition of the hipster as a beatnik, delinquent, or banal eccentric. The Negro must live on a precarious ridge between order and violence, Mailer asserted. "Second class citizen" is a silly euphemism covering the fact that his skin color makes the Negro peculiarly vulnerable to police arrest, on one level, and to rejection from approved social institutions, on the other, if he would live anything but a strictly segregated existence. Under such constant threats, he is, ironically, uniquely able to resort to violence. He has been conditioned to be "hip"; he has an outlaw's freedom denied any white man. The hipster has come into being in a post-war American society which has increasingly resembled the repressive environment the Negro has known all his life. If the hipster and the Negro cannot submit to the full canon of American middle-class respectability (and they should not, Mailer insists), they must live outside it and defy it as meaningfully as they can.

As Mailer, Griffin, and Ellison had done before him, Hersey recognized that writing on the racial question had to be for the sake of something beyond pity, shock, or even shame. Therefore, he wrote on the abstract idea of racial identity: what would it mean for any man to be a member of a subjugated race? How would the will to live express itself under such a condition? What would there be of heroism, cunning, cowardice, or mockery to shade such perserverance? Gradually, Hersey developed the idea for *White Lotus*. White Americans would be transported as slaves to China, after the "Yellow Empire" had conquered the United States at an indeterminate date. In the course of several years, they would repeat the history of the Negro in America.

The novel would be told from the point of view of one of the slaves, and Hersey's main source for developing such a point of view would have to be the many stories of human survival which he had reported over the years since he had first joined the staff of the Luce publications. Those stories freshest in his mind as he worked on *White Lotus* were collected for publication in 1963 in *Here To Stay*. *Hiroshima* was included in this collection, and, for reasons already evident from the consideration of this book in an earlier chapter, the story of how six people reacted to total calamity suggested many ways in which white Americans would behave if they were suddenly enslaved, not the least of which would be to decide whether survival under such conditions was worthwhile at all. Especially toward the end of *Hiroshima*, among Hersey's observations of his subjects' feelings a year after the bomb, was he able to perceive the attitudes of subject peoples toward their conquerors.

Less obvious leads may be found in stories that range from the plight of an old lady in the Connecticut floods of 1955 to John F. Kennedy's life-saving exploits as commander of the shattered PT-109. In "Over the Mad River,"[3] Mrs. Kelley, of Winsted, Connecticut, chooses to be rescued from her tenement apartment threatened by flood waters when the perilous means of rescue seem far more dangerous than the alternative of staying in the building. Nor is there any apparent explanation for the motives of the profane young steeplejack who rescues her. Ordinary, unheroic people had been thrust into a situation calling for their tenacity. In "Journey Toward a Sense of Being

Treated Well," Hersey describes in detail the dangerous and
tedious escape, shortly after the suppression of the Hungarian
Revolt in 1956, of the Fekete family from Budapest to the
Austrian border. Here the struggle for survival is measured out
in coffee-spoons: catching the right train, finding a sedative for
a hysterical child, being passed from house to house ahead of
the police. In *White Lotus*, Hersey would not need to rely
solely on historical accounts of the Underground Railroad for
his descriptions of fugitive-slave traffic.

The Kennedy story is entitled "A Sense of Community," a
term explained in a note attached to the article he had written
twenty years before for the *New Yorker*:

> It is the tale of a young man's discovery of his inner funds of
> resourcefulness, optimism, and stamina, and it exemplifies better
> than any other story in this book, the courage-giving force of a
> sense of community. Here the community was a small crew, Ken-
> nedy's own; as commanding officer of a Patrol Torpedo boat, he
> was responsible for the ten of his twelve men who survived the
> duty toward them—so that his thoughts and anxieties and actions
> were all turned outward from himself—may well have been what
> saved both him and them. (85)

This sense of community had already been a major theme of
The Wall, as it appeared in Noach Levinson's creation of a
family within the ghetto. It is repeated throughout *White Lotus*.

The story in *Here To Stay* which provides the greatest number
of suggestions for *White Lotus* is "Tattoo Number 107,907,"[4]
the account of how "Alfred Stirmer" survived Auschwitz. Stirmer's fight for survival goes on for several years and is many-
sided and sometimes unheroic. Stirmer is introduced to living
in Berlin in the first years of the war; a proscribed Jew, he is
permitted to work at the sufferance of the Third Reich. He must
walk several miles to his job because Jews are not permitted to
use public transportation. He, his wife, and his three-year-old
son must live in a room apartment by order of the state; they
may not attend plays, concerts, or other public entertainments.
If this former law student had not been a competent welder, his
family would long since have been off to the camps. The day
finally comes, however, when the Nazis' anti-Semitic policies
sweep away even this much protection; and the family is
herded to raidroad cars and the journey east.

Inevitably, they are separated when they reach camp. Leave-taking is abrupt, and Stirmer is faced with the likelihood that he will never see his wife or child again. He shares the bitter experience that had been the lot of Negro slaves at auction centuries before in America and would be the lot of the characters in *White Lotus* who are repeatedly cut off from family, from friends, and from any of the security that a person may gain from his voluntary association with other human beings. Many of Stirmer's fellow prisoners lose the will to survive at this point, one of the countless junctures in Hersey's works where readers must forcibly consider what would be the terms of their own survival.

Alfred Stirmer finds himself marching off to work details, keeping an eye out for chances at lighter work, and making fine calculations about how to preserve his energies. While he is partly inspired by the stubborn conviction that Germany will lose the war, that there is a limit of months or years upon what he must endure, he has no idea of what will happen to him when it is all over. Will he fall in love again? Will he ever have another three-year-old son? Will he return to a reconstructed Germany or go away to Palestine or to the United States? Or is he surviving merely for the sake of revenge?

Beyond Alfred Stirmer's anxieties, Hersey implies the following question: can a human being will to live toward utter uncertainty? Can he will to live with no other promise offered him than merely being alive the next moment and, with the promise renewed, the following moment? Here there is no question of a better life or even another life. Hersey's readers might consider that Alfred Stirmer's story has provided answers beyond even those to be found in a rereading of *Hiroshima;* for Stirmer did survive Auschwitz, was found by American ground forces in Germany, and told his story to Hersey some years later in Connecticut. His story ends with his being found by American troops; nothing is said about what he had gained for having survived.

Two years later, *White Lotus* was published. It is Hersey's longest novel to date, longer even than *The Wall;* and it calls for a special understanding beyond that exacted from readers of *The Wall, The Marmot Drive,* or *A Single Pebble.* Hersey's intention is disarmingly simple in *White Lotus*: to make white readers feel what life would be like if they were members of an oppressed racial minority. His method is extremely complicated.

The story is the first-person narrative of an American girl transported to slavery in China; it is told retrospectively from the moment in which she finds herself a member of a non-violent civil rights movement in which she assumes the "sleeping bird" posture of resistance and faces the bigoted governor of a "hardcore" province. Hersey allows himself no such inspired mechanism as the Levinson archive in *The Wall*. The whole history of a subjugated race (incredibly compressed into a few years) is told solely in terms of this girl's experiences. While she must be bright enough to tell such a story, her narrative must also reflect the debasement of her people.

Hersey's imagined circumstances alone strain belief; characterization of White Lotus herself is a nearly impossible task. The novel could not have been written neatly, unless by those writers of unpremised absurdity who would disdain explanations. One may imagine *White Lotus* in the manner of James Purdy's *Malcolm* or Joseph Heller's *Catch-22*: the story would begin in the middle of a slave's routine and lead toward his beheading with a few fragmentary admissions along the way concerning the slave's skin color and his master's. If Hersey's story had been set nowhere and had undertaken to say nothing, it would have had a good chance for critical approval. Instead, Hersey's success in *White Lotus* must be measured by the standards William Faulkner (and others before him) have set for noble failures. Hersey has tried to do far more than disdain or a fashionably wry grimace permit a writer to do.

The circumstances do strain belief. The reader must fix the fall of the United States to the "Yellow Empire" at some time in recent history, perhaps the 1920's. World War I has not taken place, however; nor has much recognizable history except for a few technological developments. There are Hollywood movies and transcontinental highways traveled over by Pierce Arrows; the Arizona tribal village, in which the chronicle begins, owns a half-track bulldozer. Once the slaves arrive in China, there is no mention of movies or Pierce Arrows; all farm chores are done with hand tools. Uncaptured American survivors of the defeat live much as their African counterparts may have in the fifteenth and sixteenth centuries. Roving agents from white-slave syndicates capture them whenever the markets in the "Yellow Empire" run low and send them across the Pacific on slave ships.

The unnamed girl who will become White Lotus is marched

along with her tribe over a route roughly that of US highways
66 and 70 through Palm Springs and the San Fernando Valley
to her embarkation point. There are brief rebellions aboard the
slave ship that are quelled by simple, absolutely final, reprisals.
With some haste, Hersey establishes the hopelessness of the
American's enslavement. Nowhere in the book is there a back-to-
America movement; there are also no revival and seemingly no
memory of an American homeland. There is no hint of American
Ghanas to rise some day, nor is there even an American Liberia
proposed in the course of the story.

These facts help to confirm that Hersey is dealing with the
abstract question of what it feels like to be a member of an
oppressed racial minority, despite the numerous parallels that
may be drawn between the story of the whites in his novel and
the history of American Negroes from the slave ships to the
"sit-ins." The Negro experience must be the pattern of much of
the Hersey story, but he is not simply engaged in re-creating
that experience in another time and place with people of a
different color. His "author's note" expressed his intentions with
a certain honest vagueness: "This work is not intended as
prophecy; perhaps it should be thought of as an extended dream
about the past, for in this story, as in dreams, invisible masks
cover and color known faces, happenings are vaguely familiar
yet "different," time is fluid, and there is a haunting feeling that
people just like us, and we ourselves, have lived in such strange
places as these. It is, in short, a history that might have been, a
tale of an old shoe on a new foot" (ix).

Much of the "old shoe" aspect of the novel, at least to Hersey,
comes from the Chinese setting. White Lotus and her fellow
Arizonians and Californians arrive in a China that has many
superficial similarities to the land Hersey remembered from his
childhood. Precise history is again dismissed: this "Yellow Empire" is untouched by Sun Yat-sen's revolution, nor is it a
fanciful representation of present-day China, with Hersey coyly
re-establishing the capital in Peiping. There is a remembered
China in street scenes, landscapes, and households: detailed
memories of a man who had seen these things as a child of
American missionaries and revisited some of them later as a
journalist when he wrote of "Red Pepper Village." There are
vivid reproductions of speech and customs that antedate Sun
Yat-sen and linger into the Communist era. There is, to give

Hersey special credit, a very skillful exploitation of something that only a foreign child could adequately sense about a strange people: their own feeling of belonging to a superior civilization. The Chinese side of *White Lotus* is interpreted by the child of "white devils," however politely they may have been received as Christian missionaries. Therefore, the slave psychology of the transported Americans may be more accessible to a writer of Hersey's background than it would be to an American writer who had never grown up in a compound. It is, thus, completely misleading to see the novel as only an extended parable of the Negro experience in the United States. Features of that experience are used as the basis of themes and incidents in *White Lotus* because they have become the most vivid tokens available of the abstraction that is Hersey's subject.

In the novel, White Lotus's existence in China is painstakingly traced through six stages: three, as a slave; three, as an emancipated white. While Hersey has introduced with minimal exposition White Lotus as a strange sort of American teen-ager living in circumstances unlike those in any sovereign America of his readers' imaginations, he develops laboriously her full identity as a subjugated white. Not only must she come to writhe in her white inferiority, but she must slowly acknowledge the superiority of the yellow conquerors. She must become a white person striving to attain the values of the yellows. Her speech takes on the figurativeness of the sayings of the yellows. Thrust into a slave's routine, she accepts the full fact of yellow mastery. She comes to see whites as the yellows see them. Only the heartlessness and ignorance of a reviewer could suggest that these changes embody a "point that could be expressed in an epigram."[5]

The girl's first masters are Peking aristocrats who seem to offer an easy berth. She is the house slave of Big Shen, a member of the College of Literature, whose wife typifies the formal daintiness associated with women of her class and thus begins the theme of white coarseness. While her chores are scarcely back-breaking, White Lotus gets a full measure of the slave's ignominy in the series of dully painful episodes through which she comes to know her place. She addresses her master and mistress as "Big Venerable" and "Big Madame," scurries to perform the slightest service, and begins to seek the small fugitive pleasures afforded slaves in back alley taverns. She learns new words, accepts her new life as though she had never had another, and generally lives by the "slaves' basic law": "No matter how frightened you are before a yellow person, no matter how angry, no matter even how happy, control your face and body; show no feeling; have a face as impassive as a figure painted on a china bowl" (88).

She learns that there are slave values and yellow values. Hersey's task at this point not merely involves the description of her absorption of slave values but also her gradual acceptance of yellow ones as an ultimate good toward which she will strive. Indeed, white readers may find nothing more difficult to accept in *White Lotus* than the unchallenged premise that these white slaves strive to integrate with a yellow society. There is none of the separatist sentiment that has marked the Black Nationalist movements in recent American history. To make this total debasement of white racial pride completely convincing, Hersey might have tried to suggest the state of America that led to the Yellow Empire's triumph; for he implies that within less than a generation whatever that civilization had become had reverted to something like African tribalism.

White Lotus's back-alley excursions lead her to witness rituals of rebellion among her fellow slaves: empty oaths standing surrogate for violence because the whites never go beyond petty theft or malingering. When mysterious fires break out in the city, the slaves become scapegoats. Familiar stereotypes flourish as the masters spread rumors of slave revolts. Being bad, the slaves think, is the only revenge. The Arizona farm boy, once named Gabriel but now called Nose, titillates Chinese matrons when he is brought to trial. Legends of sexual potency are attributed to the whites, and they are promiscuous in a desultory way. White Lotus loses her virginity without regret or excitement.

The slaves are suspected of being in league with the Moslems, who are making vague threats at the borders of the Yellow Empire. Finally, after a panicky season of trials and beheadings, such enlightened masters as Big Shen conclude that the slaves are only fit to work as field hands, and White Lotus is sold at auction to be transported to Honan. Two slavery episodes remain, both illustrating plantation life. Hersey borrows nothing from Harriet Beecher Stowe or Thomas Nelson Page; instead, he centers these sections on an abortive rebellion and a movement that roughly resembles the Underground Railroad of the 1850's. The rebellion is undertaken by an illiterate religious fanatic named Peace, who madly quotes scripture to his followers: "Thou shalt not touch these locks for it is given unto me to deliver Israel out of the hands of the Philistines"; "with the jawbone of an ass will I slay a thousand" (249).

White Lotus becomes one of Peace's several handmaidens with as easy complaisance as she had mustered in the sordid tavern revels in Peking. More fortunately for her, she also meets a slave named Smart, who begins to teach her how to read. Again, Hersey's treatment of the level of white American culture, whatever its absence of a historical fixed point, astonishes the reader; for White Lotus, who at least read movie magazines back in Arizona, is treated as if she were completely illiterate and as if her grasping the meaning of Chinese characters were her great breakthrough to the only enlightenment the world had to offer. Of course, this condition is exactly what he means—further proof that he is working mightily to make every implication of his abstraction concrete, a task that could not be turned off in an epigram.

As White Lotus picks up her characters, the reader is given several glimpses of the primitiveness of field-hand culture by the mention of folk medicines, fish fries, and the plaintive question, "Was our white God himself a slave?" Peace's rebellion is thwarted by God's own torrents inundating farms and villages and driving his far-flung co-conspirators to hide in their hovels. When details of the rebels' plans come to light, another mass auction takes place, and White Lotus is dispatched to a small landholder in Shantung. This last master is the meanest of all, grubbing away at his pitiful acres as wretchedly as his own slaves. As the work gets less and less bearable, the tension is increased by rumors of abolitionist movements in the north and impending civil war throughout the empire. (Hersey does not mention details of this war, nor does he allude to any counterparts of Lincoln or Jefferson Davis.) An Uncage-the-Finches society has sprung up in the Northern Capital; but, as politicians temporize to avoid the conflict, there is also a Clip-the-Wings edict.

Life at Hua's farm goes on in narrowing cycles of weariness and debasement. White Lotus crudely chases a neighboring slave named Dolphin, an uninteresting, self-centered lecher.

Farmer Hua also asserts his liege lord rights over her unresponding body. She marries Dolphin in a slave ceremony, becomes pregnant, miscarries, and then is abandoned as her husband tries to escape. At her most downcast point, the girl meets a sincere yellow abolitionist, Salt Inspector Feng, whose official duties are a cover for his activities within "the Kingdom of the Mole." Thus having been reached by a Northern do-gooder, White Lotus is spirited away at night under the protection of still another man who is "ashamed of his yellow skin" and courts martyrdom by the risks he takes in bringing his charges to safety.

Then the slave years are over, and White Lotus and her companions enter upon new lives as "free" citizens of the Yellow Empire. The novel thereby enters within the present-day concerns of its readers, but more than half its pages have been spent in the effort to define the condition of the subjugated race. Freedom is predictably bitter and disillusioning for the refugees. Yellow urban masses are incensed over a war fought for freedom of the "hogs," and the government has been compelled to institute selective service ("the Number Wheel"). White Lotus's newest lover, Rock, fails to get called up; and the couple work in a white orphanage that becomes the target of yellow reprisals when things go badly in the "pig lovers war." After the war finally dissipates into an indecisive victory for the government, White Lotus and Rock leave Peking to begin a new life in the "humility belt" of Hunan. The two most important sections of the novel follow.

Life in the humility belt roughly parallels the existence of Negro tenant farmers in the most deprived sections of the American South (again without any reference to fixed dates). White Lotus and Rock settle in the village of Brass Mouth Chang, who is determined to "teach some of the world's better ways" to culturally deprived whites. White Lotus sets up a school, where she subversively teaches Chinese classics to white peasant children. (Hersey never capitalizes "white" at any point in this novel, but as he proceeds to describe the rehabilitation of the race, one may well wonder why he should not.)

White peasants accept usurious landholding conditions where they are at the complete mercy of Lung, the local suzerain. When they fail to deliver their quotas, they are subject to the meanest confiscations and exactions, even to the jars in which they have hoarded their own excrements. Because White Lotus is literate and her husband is a harder bargainer than his fellows, White Lotus is subject to the constant suspicion leveled at "smart pigs." One day her school is raided by hooded members of The Hall, who terrify her pupils, smash every object in sight, and later return with a decree that cites a pre-war law which prohibits any education whatsoever for white children. White Lotus submits.

> Then, when it was over, I told the children that the yellows were closing our school.

> Ayah! My children were white children, indeed! not a sign, not a sigh. No emotion whatsoever. Guarded, cautious, hooded eyes. No comment, no protest, no questions. (526)

The redoubtable Rock begins drinking heavily. Both he and White Lotus turn jealous and promiscuous. Rock almost kills a neighbor who had slept with White Lotus, even though Rock had raised no objection at the time and had, in fact, taken the neighbor's wife. In the midst of their torpor, the couple's old Peking friend, Groundnut, turns from beggar into priest and sets up a lucrative Fundamentalist temple. He, however, turns from further cupidity upon the arrival of a genuine evangelist, Runner; it is this man who begins to pronounce the maxims which lead to the eventual movement of non-violent protest. Meanwhile, the mission of White Lotus and Rock to uplift their race is an abysmal failure, and the couple flee the rural provinces to seek their fortunes in Shanghai.

"The Enclave," the last portion of the novel, considers the most immediately familiar material to American readers, for Hersey describes in it his fictional counterpart of the Negro's great migration to the industrial North and his settlement in the several Harlems of Northern cities. Shanghai ("Up-from-the-Sea") is a city of wonder and modern times. The peasant whites are dazzled by skyscrapers along the Bund and by the possibilities of creature comforts for themselves in the Enclave. Soon enough they learn that employment is rigidly restricted. White men may become ricksha boys or dock coolies; white women, a few lucky ones, may work in the silk mills. The most fortunate of both sexes may become house servants. But there are the rare whites who have done remarkably well: the very few professional men;

the racketeers; and, at the very top, the impresarios of the For-getfulness Hong, who run lotteries and opium dens.

White Lotus works in a silk mill and grasps too easily the Enclave's opportunities for white happiness. Always attractive to males of her own race, she schemes endlessly to pass as a "Chinkty," which is more than a mere round of hair-straighten-ing and yellowing cosmetics; true "quality" comes from mimick-ing the delicacy of yellow manners and by discreetly surprising her yellow acquaintances with her literacy. She appeals to yellow liberals who gather in salons to hear recitations by white poets, and one of the starry-eyed Chinese falls in love with her.

This episode might have been an interesting end for the novel, except that the heroine is given a last glimpse of the future of mass action for her race. Groundnut has brought his religious following to Shanghai and has been perfecting non-violent resistance by creating the "sleeping bird gesture," an excruciating stance in which the demonstrator raises one foot to his knee and gazes upon the ground. Even Rock has been won away to this group from the desperation of trying to "pass" or from the open revolt of the "Give-Us-The-Rice" campaign. The recruitment of White Lotus gives the movement its most effective "bird"; and, after a few successes in Shanghai, the group moves on to the hard-core provinces. So the novel ends where it had begun with White Lotus facing the provincial governor in the center of a field of bystanders. She is the first to speak. "Virtuous wisdom, gentle hand," she says softly; and the governor turns away silent. White Lotus stands her ground; she is now convinced that the races must speak to each other.

But, as police approach to arrest her, a more disturbing thought presses upon her:

> Looking at the retreating Governor's back, I have a thought that floods me, at the very time when perhaps I should be giving way to a blessed sense of victory, instead with a fear as puzzling as any I have felt in all my life up to now:
> What if someday we are the masters and they are the under-dogs? (683)

Thus, Hersey ends *White Lotus* by appealing to the universality of his theme of racial identity.

White Lotus won little approval from early reviewers. It is a long, detailed novel in a period of shorter masterpieces; but, worse, it proceeds abstractly and detachedly into a subject that is being treated with head-on vehemence by almost every other writer. The only novel remotely like it is Ellison's *The Invisible Man*, which adds a terrifying humor to the extraordinary vividness of its sweeping account of racial identity. It is like Ellison's book in seeking to define what racial difference means and in pursuing the definition through a broad sweep of social history. It lacks the humor of *The Invisible Man* or the evidence of controlled and exploited anger, which, in turn, distinguishes that novel from the fiction of James Baldwin and Richard Wright.

Obviously, *White Lotus* must differ from the work of any of these men because of the limitations of Hersey's background. The racial novel by a white writer may have to be written about the white race, whether it is a novel of pride or guilt, compassion or bewilderment; but it should be an actual white race, whose story may be less meaningful or ambitious than that of the imagined white American slaves of *White Lotus*. To the extent that Hersey can convince us of debased white awe before yellow manners—to the extent that he can successfully build upon the memory of his own foreignness in an earlier China—he approaches the requirements of that hypothetical white novel.

On the other hand, despite his much larger intentions, he may have tried the only way by which a white writer could feelingly describe certain conditions of contemporary Negro life. Because the action is reduced to a comparatively few years, he cannot convince us that he has drawn anything like a close parallel. The American Negro, except in a few tragic instances, is far better off than White Lotus and her friends; at least, he has experienced a far more complex spectrum of triumphs and deprivations than the novel could possibly recount. Yet, had Hersey made this book subtler still, he would have made it far longer and, inevitably, much more tedious. *White Lotus* is a little longer than *The Wall*, and neither book moves as swiftly as many books much longer. Both novels depend on the author's amassing a huge amount of historical and cultural detail if their subjects are to be presented at all honestly. *The Wall* has the advantage of first-hand historical reality over *White Lotus* and is, therefore, that much more vivid.

In reading *White Lotus*, one must never forget that the novel began with an abstraction and that the novelist was trying to do something that no other white writer had attempted. Faced with comparable situations, other writers have become satirists, and perhaps Hersey might have written a better book if he had refined the method that he applied to his exposé of American educational abuses. Instead, operating within a thoroughly fanciful situation, he has done his best to write a thoroughly realistic novel. Such realism is not just the technical question of verisimilitude; it is the art of the naturalist applied to an anti-utopia.

To the extent that the reader yields to fancy or to the discovery of a general truth at the expense of specific revelations, *White Lotus* is a fascinating book. However, almost any preconception that the reader may have about racial identity will qualify his acceptance of this novel. It is hardly possible, in the 1960's, to keep circumstantial parallels between history and Hersey's fiction within the tenuous framework of the "extended dream" demanded by the author. Nor is it easy to be patient through the painstaking exposition which must make an imagined yellow civilization as real as the imaginary white slaves. The historical importance of *White Lotus* will surely grow, however, as future writers treat Hersey's abstraction in other ways.

CHAPTER 8

Hersey in Mid-Career

I *The Unclassifiable Writer*

JOHN HERSEY is clearly in the middle of his career: an energetic writer with disciplined work habits, he is both blessed and cursed by the compulsion to deal with a wide variety of subjects and to attempt as great a diversity of fictional forms. In this respect, he is a little like John Dos Passos, who is so difficult to pin down as a novelist, historian, or reporter that one may willingly accept his own definition of his works as "contemporary chronicles."[1] Very much like the later Dos Passos, Hersey has met the fate which awaits unclassifiable writers on most levels of American literary criticism of the 1960's. Reviewers, upon reading something like *The Marmot Drive* after having read *The Wall*, despair over a broken pattern; and the journal critics ignore Hersey altogether or mention him deprecatingly as a foil to their hard-working wit.

The reviewers of *The Marmot Drive* might simply have accepted this least of Hersey's novels as an indication of the unpredictable variety which has marked all his work. They might have realized that Hersey was not one of the self-conscious aspirants preoccupied with what could be properly undertaken by a novelist in the 1950's, but simply a writer wondering what *he* would do next. He may have begun to prove, at that point, that a novelist can do worse than begin as a journalist—a fact that may not seem to require special assertion after such examples as Stephen Crane and Ernest Hemingway. Yet, assuming Hersey to be a different case from Crane and Hemingway because he wrote for such untypical media as *Time* and *Life*, it must be argued that his superficial assimilation of events and ideas was at least balanced by his constant exposure to them and, above all, by his professional commitment to report what he had seen.

The reporter keeps on going; but the novelist, who has begun his writing career as a novelist, is prone to such self-conscious interruptions as may come from sudden leisure or sudden doubts. Hersey after *The Marmot Drive* was not in the same position that Norman Mailer had been after the hostile reviews of *The Barbary Shore,* nor as James Jones would be in the years between *From Here to Eternity* and *Some Came Running.*[2] Hersey was not stalled as Mailer was by the insufficiency of a political viewpoint; by the same token, he had no comparable point of departure for defining a personal philosophy. Unlike Jones, he was not an overnight celebrity whose next book was written under the pressure of his dizzying reputation. He was less fortunate, perhaps, than Saul Bellow or Wright Morris, who developed their work on bases which would not be shaken by ideological commitments or by the glare of publicity. They may have been better off than Hersey for having known precisely what they could do and what they would write about.

The central question in judging what Hersey has accomplished as a writer is "what is he likely to go on to do?" How does one measure a writer who cannot be subtitled? "John Hersey: Novelist of Contemporary History" and "War Correspondent into Novelist" are not very arresting and can lead to little more than a summary of his work. There are no lines to be taken from his writing, no fine allusive phrases that can serve as a casual metaphor for his career. He offers no patently developed "world view" or system of thought. But for anyone who would merely entitle his essay "John Hersey: *Time*style Novelist," and resent the man's inaccessibility to critical fashion, there is a challenge which should not be evaded. Hersey is a skillful writer who is devoted to the profound treatment of several of the most serious topics his era affords. He cannot be ignored because he treats these topics directly. If critical essays are not necessary to interpret his lucid writing, he should be no less esteemed.

II *Hersey and the Classifiers: A Short Summary*

Some understanding of how Hersey has been judged or why he has been ignored may come from a brief consideration of criticism of American fiction since 1945. Critical assessment has been a weary exercise in discontent broken by a few reversions to enthusiasm as individual critics settle for the few writers about whom they are willing to hedge. This tone has prevailed in reviews (with a few significant exceptions)[3] whenever they have not been unreservedly hostile or despairing. Happily, a few longer critical studies have been more scrutinizing.

As early as 1951, John Aldridge plotted the long odds that new writers faced in matching the previous war generation of Hemingway, Fitzgerald, and Dos Passos. Writing as their sympathetic contemporary in *After the Lost Generation,* Aldridge described the first efforts of eleven men as hopefully as he could; but he finished his study with a pessimistic survey of the environment that awaited their further work.[4] Seven years later, after essays and reviews and a more petulant second book by Aldridge had all but dismissed the writing of fiction except for the sake of its being criticized, Granville Hicks mustered ten novelists who made their own statements about their craft—and he pointedly titled his collection *The Living Novel.*[5] Few books since 1945 have been more undeservedly ignored; the general notice (a rather hypocritical one) was that these people were derelict to have taken time out from writing their novels.

In 1961 *Radical Innocence* appeared, an overwhelmingly scholarly assessment of thirteen American writers that was complete with a long résumé of their contemporaries and an even longer essay on historical influences and critical positions of the post-war years. Ihab Hassan described the rebel-victim (whether fictional hero or practicing novelist) as recoiling from his encounters with the world into the innocence lying in his roots in order to gain strength for a second round with experience. It was an inspired means of explaining the writers that Hassan selected, all of whom deserve the judicious attention he has given them. Bellow, Donleavy, McCullers, and Swados, as four of the thirteen, suggest this critic's range. Yet Hassan's very metaphor returns one to John Hersey and to the bewildering state of his literary reputation, for Hersey's writing career is a vivid example of the process described in *Radical Innocence.* Hersey is a writer of sheltered origins (the missionary compound and the private schools) thrust before the most appalling circumstances of World War II. He recoils to the most abiding premise of his innocence: a belief in the human will to survive. His eleven books follow. The foregoing chapters of this study have traced the outlines of Hersey's encounter in terms of what

he witnessed from Chungking to Warsaw and the well of
earnest intention at his roots which provoked his untheoretical,
seldom subtle, liberal and humanistic response in his work.

Why, then, is Hersey not considered with the American
writers who most interest the critics? For one thing, his encounters with experience (whether his characters' or his own)
are less complicated by introversion than Saul Bellow's—or even
Norman Mailer's. Hersey's works lack those fascinating and ex-
asperating digressions into self-doubt, articulated apathy, or
near-madness that mark the novels by or about individuals who
are less certain of the possibility of human survival. Hersey is
an affirmative writer, and his affirmations seem unfashionably
direct. Their directness may lead one to ignore the honesty and
thoroughness with which they have been conceived.

The Wall, above all his books, illustrates the special nature of
his achievement. This novel of the Warsaw ghetto was of
imagined happenings that approximated the historical record.
In them he illustrated men's determination to survive the most
wretched of circumstances, along with the strength and even the
joy born of their hardships; and he showed minutely the changes
in human character that can come from a small occurrence in
the midst of a great event. He might have imagined as well the
response of a victim in terms of self-destruction or retreat into
apathy or absurdity, but he was confronted by the fact that the
Jews of the Warsaw ghetto fought back and zealously preserved
precious human values and that some of them actually survived.
Therefore, as a novelist, he concluded *The Wall* with an honest
affirmation. When he has Rachel Apt ask: "*Nu*, what is the plan
for tomorrow?" he is trying to do what Tolstoy did in having
Konstantin Levin make the simple assertion that spoke for the
end of his spiritual struggles: "Do I not know that that is
infinite space, and that it is not a round arch? But, however I
screw up my eyes and strain my sight, I cannot see it not round
and not bounded, and in spite of my knowing about infinite
space, I am incontestably right when I see a solid blue dome,
and more right than when I strain my eyes to see beyond it."[6]

For the sake of his future literary reputation, Hersey should
have written *The Marmot Drive* before *The Wall*. He would
then have produced a comparatively private, obscure book to
prove that he wanted to be known as a novelist, as one within
a genre in the post-war world. Instead, *The Wall* followed too

soon upon the impression he had made between 1942 and 1946 when *A Bell for Adano* and *Hiroshima* defined too clearly his strengths and limitations. No one has ever said that *Hiroshima* was an inferior work, but its excellence should not have stigmatized Hersey. Aldridge cites *Hiroshima* as a superior *New Yorker* piece beside what he considers the meretricious *New Yorker* aspect of Irwin Shaw's *The Young Lions*.[7] Hassan includes *Hiroshima* and *The Wall* in a series with *The Diary of Anne Frank* and the Air Force transcripts on American prisoners of war in Korea as documents which "give forth the collective *de profundis* cry of our century."[8] Not one, but two superior pieces of Hersey's journalism! Neither critic mentions him again in these seminal studies of post-war fiction. Norman Mailer, in *Advertisements for Myself* and in later articles for *Esquire*, has something to say about almost all of his writing contemporaries from Saul Bellow to Calder Willingham; but he never mentions Hersey. In a *Paris Review* interview, Truman Capote refers to Hersey offhandedly (but not deprecatingly) as a "plain style guy."[9]

But Hersey has not lacked praise. Tributes to *the man* have been written since his early reporting, and those to his work are not restricted to newspaper reviews and the *Book-of-the-Month-Club News*. It is precisely the personal praise, though, which has annoyed some of the serious critics. Norman Cousins reports that Dr. Fujii, of *Hiroshima*, believed "your President Lincoln" must have been like Hersey;[10] and Leslie Fiedler remarks in the *Partisan Review*: "I am never sure who should be despised, Hersey for being so pious or me for being appalled by that piety."[11] Fiedler wasn't uncertain for long. Having settled on as pejorative a term as he could for the writer's earnestness, he despised Hersey.

Fiedler's comments formed part of a review he devoted to a despairing statement about the contemporary American novel, and it followed another essay in the same issue in which a less famous critic ended a bright appreciation of Evelyn Waugh by saying: "Until the conventions of the written language have become more accessible to our daily speech, America will continue to present us with writers who, though of the highest talents and intentions, are largely brilliant and inspired amateurs."[12] A magnificent irony makes this number of *Partisan Review* a keepsake as, cheek by jowl with these obituaries of the novel, the editors saw fit to run Saul Bellow's *Seize the Day*. As one sees Hersey, on this occasion, at the center of a much larger target, it is instructive to know that a social novel, even one so short and fabular as *A Single Pebble*, was singled out for special derision.

Two years later, Maxwell Geismar perceptively noted that Hersey was not the novelist for a time in which "social themes" were suspect.[13] He stood to be attacked, therefore, by journal critics who had retreated to safer questions of taste. Eight years after having reviewed *The Wall* "a trifle fervently," Geismar saw the novel as a welcome throwback to a literary tradition concerned with social justice that included Frank Norris's *The Octopus* and John Steinbeck's *The Grapes of Wrath*. Such a concern far outweighed, for Geismar, the weakness he saw in Hersey's characterization of people in terms of the situation in which he found them, rather than in and for themselves. But Geismar still found something to admire in both *The Marmot Drive* and *A Single Pebble*. Whatever Fiedler and others might object to in Hersey's piety, Geismar approved the signs of a conscience going against the popular grain.

III *Conclusion: Something Other than a Novelist?*

Geismar's estimate of Hersey is just. He is one of many significant writers in a period of unusually diverse talents. Neither he nor any of his contemporaries will ever loom over a generation as Faulkner and Hemingway have done. Lists of these contemporaries could begin with Wright Morris or Saul Bellow or J. D. Salinger or Hersey, and then go through at least as long and as generally praiseworthy a roster as Malcolm Cowley arranged for his own generation in the appendix to *Exile's Return*. Hersey might stand among these newer writers as Thornton Wilder did among those born in the 1890's: as an unclassifiable talent heedless of genre in the production of works bearing little similarity to the accepted "classics" of the age. Hersey has written nothing so strange as Wilder's *The Skin of Our Teeth*, so plainly perfect as *Our Town*, or so rigidly a fable as *The Bridge of San Luis Rey*; his resemblance to Wilder is circumstantial—the reassuring circumstance of diverse talents within their respective generations.

One cannot reasonably predict what Hersey will do next or what he will finally achieve. He began flashily in *A Bell for Adano* with elementary skills in storytelling and with a small facility for assimilating ideas into fiction. In no way did this book foreshadow *The Wall.* His greatest novel testifies to the study which informs it and demonstrates that, in such a study, a writer may learn more of human character than he had imagined possible when he sets himself the task of absorbing documents. *The Wall* is certainly the best example among all his works of a subject finding its necessary form; and it remains —after fifteen years—still the best augury of what Hersey may finally accomplish.

The Marmot Drive, his most mysterious work, is less interesting than most such mysteries. The reader assumes that it must be dealing with a contemporary social problem—possibly with some flaw in the national character—only because this murky study in feminine psychology is pitted with allusion to the condition of the times. *A Single Pebble* is a simple fable of East and West told with a welcome clarity after *The Marmot Drive.* In *A Bell for Adano* Hersey had felt compelled to tell his reader at the outset that Victor Joppolo was a good man who stood for an everlasting peace, but he was capable in *A Single Pebble* of letting his reader proceed with the central character toward a much more rewarding discovery. *The War Lover,* for all the mechanical awkwardness of its flashback structure, is an impressive story of wartime problems of life and death. The title character—the actual "war lover"—is less convincing than the narrator for the simple reason that Hersey, himself so obviously a "life lover," found himself suddenly with a hero so unlike the victims in the war novels of his contemporaries that one must wish he could have become more fully realized. Another Boman may, should, appear in a future Hersey novel.

Hersey's two most recent novels suggest that he may be something other than a novelist: something more, rather than something less. *The Child Buyer* is a harrowing story about an American society that permits a child to become converted into a computer. Had Swift chosen to bring his "Modest Proposal" to a vote there might have been a precise literary precedent for *The Child Buyer,* but it is doubtful if such a tale would have been compressed into anything like the form Hersey chose of the transcribed testimony of hearings before a legislative committee. Tedious as this reading experience may often be, *The Child Buyer* is generally convincing; and Hersey, after all, must deal with a much more amorphous subject than the British mistreatment of Ireland in the eighteenth century. It is incidentally astonishing to observe that the writer of the wartime dispatches and *A Bell for Adano* could develop into a capable ironist.

White Lotus recalls the travail preceding *The Wall* without so felicitous a discovery of form as Noach Levinson's archive. Perhaps no such discovery could have come from the materials at hand, or perhaps Hersey undertook the most difficult way yet conceived for writing about the question of racial identity. For the sake of understanding the immediately painful situation of the Negro in history, the reader is required to learn every small detail of its fantastic, deliberately improbable analogue of an enslaved white American minority in China. This very difficulty, however, does confirm, beyond the last despairing objection, that the author of *White Lotus* is a man of unusual vitality and complete commitment to his art and to the truth of what he has seen.

Notes and References

Chapter One

1. *Current Biography* (New York, 1944), p. 286.

2. See Mark Schorer, *Sinclair Lewis: An American Life* (New York, 1961), p. 631. His duties "consisted chiefly of taking letters, driving, buying chocolates, and typing manuscript."

3. "Letter from Peiping," *The New Yorker* (May 4, 1946), pp. 86-96; "Letter from Shanghai," *The New Yorker* (February 9, 1946), pp. 82-90; "Profiles: The Happy, Happy Beggar," *The New Yorker* (May 11, 1946), pp. 34-47; "Red Pepper Village," *Life* (August 26, 1946), pp. 92-105; "A Reporter at Large: The Communization of Crow Village," *The New Yorker* (July 27, 1946), pp. 38-47; "A Reporter in China," *The New Yorker* (May 18, 1946), pp. 59-69, and May 25, 1946, pp. 54-69.

4. *Current Biography, loc. cit.*

5. "Joe Grew, Ambassador to Japan," *Life* (July 15, 1940), pp. 76-83.

6. An American gunboat sunk in the Yangtze, above Nanking, by Japanese shells on December 12, 1937.

7. He was given a letter of commendation from Secretary of the Navy Frank Knox for his conduct in aiding the removal of wounded marines at the battle of the Matanikau River, Guadalcanal.

8. "The Battle of the River," *Life* (November 23, 1942), pp. 99-116.

9. "Experience by Battle," *Life* (December 27, 1943), p. 51.

10. Author of the widely read *Guadalcanal Diary* (New York, 1943).

11. "Survival," *The New Yorker* (June 17, 1944), pp. 31-43. Reprints of "Survival" were distributed widely during Mr. Kennedy's first successful election campaign for Congress in 1946.

12. The "real" Joppolo, Frank Toscani, later dropped a $250,000 lawsuit against Hersey, after having charged that his wife became emotionally upset over reading the imaginary episode between Joppolo and Tina. Hersey had explained that the episode *was* imaginary when he presented Mrs. Toscani with a pre-publication copy of the novel. Toscani also alleged that the novel had "damaged his reputation as a civil affairs officer and as a husband." See New York *Times*, January 20, 1946, VII, p. 24, and March 14, 1946, p. 27.

13. New York *Times*, February 7, 1944, p. 11: ". . . one of the most greatly gifted young Americans now writing."

14. Diana Trilling, "Fiction in Review," *The Nation* (February 12, 1944) pp. 194-95.

15. Notably in *Rosinante to the Road Again* (New York: Doran, 1922).

16. Prescott, *op. cit.*

Chapter Two

1. "Red Pepper Village," *Life* (August 26, 1946), pp. 92-105.

2. "Letter from Peiping," *New Yorker* (May 4, 1946), p. 92.

3. *Witness* (New York, 1952), p. 498. Chambers refers to his editorship of the foreign news department in 1945-46 when "most of *Time's* European correspondents" and a "thunder clap out of Asia, from the *Time* bureau in Chungking" signed a round-robin protesting his views and demanding his removal. These men "continued to feed out news written from the viewpoint that the Soviet Union is a benevolent democracy of un-aggressive intent, or that the Chinese Communists are 'agrarian liberals.'" Chambers cited as "foremost among them," Hersey, John Scott, Charles C. Wertenbaker, Richard Lauterbach, and Theodore White.

4. A good account of Hersey's operations in writing *Hiroshima* may be found in *Newsweek*, September 9, 1946, pp. 69-71.

5. The book is dedicated to Ross and Shawn "for their considerable share in its preparation."

6. A summary of this reaction may be found in the New York *Times Book Review*, November 10, 1946, VII, p. 7.

7. New York *Times*, April 8, 1948, p. 23; April 16, 1948, p. 16; and June 15, 1948, p. 24.

8. The 1957 novel by Nevil Shute, filmed the following year by Stanley Kramer Productions.

9. *'47—The Magazine of the Year* (April, 1947), pp. 113-41.

10. *U. N. World*, I (May, 1947), 20-21, 75-76.

Chapter Three

1. His only contemporary articles on the subject were "Home to Warsaw," *Life* (April 9, 1945), pp. 16-20, and "Prisoner 339, Klooga," *Life* (October 30, 1944), pp. 72-83.

2. John Hersey, "The Mechanics of a Novel," *Yale University Library Gazette*, XXVII, 1 (July, 1952), pp. 1-11. I am indebted to Mr. Hersey for lending me his copy of this article and, later, "Intelligence: Choice and Consent," his pamphlet on education written for the Woodrow Wilson Foundation.

3. "Acknowledgements," *Mila 18* (New York: Bantam Editions, 1962).

4. David Daiches, "Review and Testament," *Commentary* (April, 1950), pp. 385-88.

5. See Mailer's *Advertisements for Myself* (New York: Putnam, 1959), pp. 27-29, an "advertisement" on this point, followed by his undergraduate short story, "A Calculus in Heaven."

6. "The Novel of Contemporary History," *The Atlantic Monthly* (November, 1959), pp. 80-84.

Chapter Four

1. "Profile: The Old Man" *The New Yorker* (January 3, 1948), pp. 28-37; (January 10, 1948), pp. 30-40; (January 17, 1948), pp. 30-41. (Baruch).

"Mr. President," *The New Yorker* (April 7, 1951), pp. 42-56; (April 14, 1951), pp. 38-53; (April 21, 1951), pp. 36-57; (April 28, 1951), pp. 36-52; (May 5, 1951), pp. 36-53. (Truman).

"A Reporter at Large: The Ingathering of the Exiles," *The New Yorker* (November 24, 1951), pp. 92-113.

"Our Far-flung Correspondents: The Kibbutz," *The New Yorker* (April 19, 1952), pp. 89-99.

2. "The Novel of Contemporary History."

3. New York *Times*, October 23, 1952, p. 19.

4. New York *Times*, September 17, 1956, p. 17.

5. William Carlos Williams, *In The American Grain*, (New York, 1956), especially pp. 63-68. ("The Voyage of the Mayflower.")

Chapter Five

1. "Experience by Battle," *Life* (December 27, 1943), p. 71.

2. Stanley Cooperman, "Willa Cather and the Bright Face of Death," *Literature and Psychology* XIII, pp. 81-87.

3. James Jones, *The Thin Red Line* (New York, 1962), vii.

4. William Butler Yeats, "An Irish Airman Foresees His Death," *Collected Poems*, New York, 1954, pp. 133-34.

Chapter Six

1. The place for such a paragraph is in the notes. Hersey's educational dossier follows: Westport (Conn.) School Study Council, 1945-50. Westport Board of Education 1950-52. Fellow, Berkeley College, Yale, 1950- . Yale University Council Committee on the Humanities, 1951-56. Fairfield (Conn.) Citizens School Study Council, 1952-56. Member, National Citizens' Commission for the Public Schools, 1954-56. Chairman, Connecticut Committee for the Gifted, 1954-57. Board

of Trustees, Putney School, 1953-56. Delegate to White House Conference on Education, 1955. Trustee, National Citizens' Council for the Public Schools, 1956-58. Member, Visiting Committee, Harvard Graduate School of Education, 1960-   . Yale University Council Committee on Yale College, 1959-64. Trustee, National Committee for Support of the Public Schools, 1962-   ; Chairman, 1965-   . Weston (Conn.) Board of Education, 1964-   .

2. "The Brilliant Jughead," *The New Yorker* (July 28, 1945), pp. 25-39.

3. "Why Do Students Bog Down on the First R?" *Life* (May 24, 1954), pp. 136-50.

4. The writer borrowed Mr. Hersey's own copy after failing to find it in two university libraries and an education department, and after getting a negative reply from the Woodrow Wilson Foundation as well.

5. *New Republic* (October 10, 1960), pp. 21-25. Margaret Halsey, "The Shortest Way with Assenters"; B. F. Skinner, "May We Have a Positive Contribution?"; Carl F. Hansen, "Educator vs. Educationist"; Robert Gorham Davis, "Arrangement in Black and White"; William Jay Smith, "The Truly Handicapped."

Chapter Seven

1. Besides *Invisible Man* (New York, 1952), consult "Hidden Name and Complex Fate," in *The Writer's Experience* (Washington, 1964), pp. 1-16. (Ellison's Gertrude Clarke Whittall Lecture given at the Library of Congress, January 6, 1964.)

2. *Black Like Me* (Boston, 1961). *The White Negro* (New York, 1957), reprinted in *Advertisements for Myself*.

3. See the bibliography for original publication dates of articles reprinted in *Here To Stay*.

4. Published for the first time in this collection, pp. 189-239.

5. *Time* (January 29, 1965), p. 96. The reviewer failed in his own epigrammatic efforts to sum up Hersey's career: "He asked for the silver tongue; he was given the golden touch. He longed to write great novels that would endure for centuries; he has written magnificent volumes of journalism that make the Book-of-the-Month Club."

Chapter Eight

1. In an interview with the present writer, June 30, 1962, to be published in *Paris Review*.

2. N. Mailer, *Advertisements for Myself*, 91-107, especially "Third Advertisement for Myself," 105-7. Nelson W. Aldrich, Jr., "The Art of

Fiction XXII: James Jones," *Paris Review*, No. 20 (Autumn-Winter, 1958-59), pp. 35-55.

3. See, for example, Alfred Kazin, "The Alone Generation," in *Contemporaries* (Boston, 1962), pp. 207-16.

4. The writers: Alfred Hayes, Robert Lowry, Vance Bourjaily, Norman Mailer, John Horne Burns, Irwin Shaw, Merle Miller, Gore Vidal, Paul Bowles, Truman Capote, and Fredric Buechner.

5. New York, 1957. The novelists: Saul Bellow, Paul Darcy Boles, John Brooks, Ralph Ellison, Herbert Gold, Mark Harris, Wright Morris, Flannery O'Connor, Harvey Swados, and Jessamyn West.

6. Leo Tolstoy, *Anna Karenina* (New York: Modern Library, 1950), p. 930.

7. Aldridge, *op. cit.*, p. 147.

8. Hassan, *op. cit.*, p. 16.

9. Malcolm Cowley (ed.), *Writers at Work: The Paris Review Interviews*, First Series (New York, 1957), p. 290.

10. "John Hersey," *Saturday Review*, (March 4, 1950), p. 15.

11. "The Novel in the Post-Political World," *Partisan Review*, XXIII (Summer, 1956), p. 362.

12. Steven Marcus, "Evelyn Waugh and the Art of Entertainment," *op. cit.*, p. 357.

13. "John Hersey: The Revival of Conscience," in *American Moderns* (New York, 1958), pp. 180-86.

Selected Bibliography

PRIMARY SOURCES

1. Books

A Bell for Adano. New York: Alfred A. Knopf, Inc., 1944.
The Child Buyer. New York: Alfred A. Knopf, Inc., 1960.
Here to Stay. New York: Alfred A. Knopf, Inc., 1963.
Hiroshima. New York: Alfred A. Knopf, Inc., 1946.
Into the Valley. New York: Alfred A. Knopf, Inc., 1943.
The Marmot Drive. New York: Alfred A. Knopf, Inc., 1953.
Men on Bataan. New York: Alfred A. Knopf, Inc., 1942.
A Single Pebble. New York: Alfred A. Knopf, Inc., 1956.
The Wall. New York: Alfred A. Knopf, Inc., 1950.
The War Lover. New York: Alfred A. Knopf, Inc., 1959.
White Lotus. New York: Alfred A. Knopf, Inc., 1965.

2. Articles and Short Stories:

"Alternatives to Apathy," *U. N. World*, I (May, 1947), 20-21, 70-76.
"AMGOT at Work," *Life* (August 23, 1943), pp. 29-31. Factual basis of *A Bell for Adano*.
"The Battle of the River," *Life* (November 23, 1942), pp. 99-116. Report on the action in the Matanikau Valley, Guadalcanal, expanded in *Into the Valley*.
"Better Classrooms for Less Money," *The Saturday Review* (September 12, 1953), pp. 18-19.
"The Brilliant Jughead," *The New Yorker* (July 28, 1945), pp. 25-39. On the U. S. Army's efforts to combat illiteracy among its personnel.
"The Death of Buchan Walsh," *The Atlantic Monthly*, CLXXVII (April, 1946), 80-86. Short story.
"Dialogue on Gorki Street," *Fortune*, XXXI (January, 1945), 149-51. Imaginary conversation with a fictitious Russian writer, who says: "I esteem other people's roads—but they must all lead to the same place and we must travel quickly on them."
"Engineers of the Soul," *Time* (October 9, 1944), pp. 99-102. On Soviet writers.
"Experience by Battle," *Life* (December 27, 1943), pp. 48-84. Text accompanying reproductions of paintings by *Life* staff artists.
"A Fable South of Cancer," *'47—The Magazine of the Year*, I (April, 1947), 113-41. Short story.
"The Hills of Nicosia," *Time* (August 9, 1943), p. 30. Cabled report on the Sicilian landings.

"Home to Warsaw," *Life* (April 9, 1945), pp. 16-20. A Polish officer returns to the ruins of his neighborhood.

"Joe Grew, Ambassador to Japan," *Life* (July 15, 1940), pp. 76-83. Hersey's first byline.

"Joe Is Home Now," *Life* (July 3, 1944), pp. 68-80. One of the first articles on returning veterans. Based on interviews. Reprinted with revision in *Here To Stay*.

"Kamikaze," *Life* (July 30, 1945), pp. 68-75. Battle of Okinawa.

"Intelligence, Choice, and Consent." A pamphlet published for the Woodrow Wilson Foundation, New York, 1959.

"Letter from Chungking," *The New Yorker* (March 16, 1946), pp. 80-87. On the departure of the Generalissimo and Mme. Chiang from the wartime capital.

"Letter from Peiping," *The New Yorker* (May 4, 1946), pp. 86-96. Prophetic article on the political situation. "No matter what the United States does, I am afraid, China is in for a long, sharp, bloody struggle."

"Letter from Shanghai," *The New Yorker* (February 9, 1946), pp. 82-90. American servicemen on liberty in China's largest and most cosmopolitan city.

"Marine in China," *Life* (May 27, 1946), pp. 17-24. Subtitled, "Butch Reynolds Meets the Strangest People."

"The Marines on Guadalcanal," *Life* (November 9, 1942), pp. 36-39.

"The Mechanics of a Novel," *The Yale University Library Gazette*, XXVII (July, 1952), 1-11. Hersey's talk on receiving the Howland Memorial Award and depositing the first draft of *The Wall* in the Yale University Library.

"Mr. President," *The New Yorker* (April 7, 1951), pp. 42-56; (April 14, 1951), pp. 38-53; (April 21, 1951), pp. 36-57; (April 28, 1951), pp. 36-52; (May 5, 1951), pp. 36-53. On Harry S. Truman.

"Mr. Secretary Marshall," *Collier's* (March 29, 1947), pp. 11-13, 48-51; (April 5, 1947), pp. 18-19, 71-73; (April 12, 1947), pp. 24, 78-81. Highly laudatory sketch of General George C. Marshall.

"Nine Men on a Four Man Raft," *Life* (November 2, 1942), pp. 54-57. Survivors of a B-17 crew interviewed aboard the USS *Hornet*.

"The Novel of Contemporary History," *The Atlantic Monthly*, CLXXXIV (November, 1949), 80-84. With "The Mechanics of a Novel," Hersey's only published statements about his work.

"Our Far-Flung Correspondents: The Kibbutz," *The New Yorker* (April 19,1952), pp. 89-99. "A baffling and trouble-making phenomenon of this century—the mutability of Socialism—is symbolized in Israel in the type of agricultural village known as the *kibbutz*."

"The Pass of the Dead One," *Life* (January 10, 1944), pp. 12-13. Reactions to a bull fight in Mexico City.

"Peggety's Parcel of Shortcomings," *The Atlantic Monthly*, CLXXXV (June, 1950), 26-30. Short story. An unloved pantry-maid tells the story of her life.

"The Pen," *The Atlantic Monthly*, CLXXVII (June, 1946), 84-87. Short story. On a missing pen which may or may not have been stolen from a U. S. Navy medical officer.

"Prisoner 339, Klooga," *Life* (October 30, 1944), pp. 72-83. Interview with a man who had just escaped the last German efforts at genocide in the Baltic States. Reprinted in *Here To Stay*.

"Profile: The Happy, Happy Beggar," *The New Yorker* (May 11, 1946), pp. 34-47. On Father Walter P. Morse and his mission in Ichang, China. "The happiest adult I had ever known."

"Profile: The Old Man," *The New Yorker* (January 3, 1948), pp. 28-37; (January 10, 1948), pp. 30-40; (January 17, 1948), pp. 30-41. On Bernard Baruch.

"PT Squadron in the South Pacific," *Life* (May 10, 1943), pp. 74-87. "Three skippers tell how they fought Jap warships." "We boat captains mostly went to Ivy League colleges . . . Another way of saying, that is, that we were snobs. To have discovered what the men in our boats were like was the best thing that could have happened to us."

"Red Pepper Village," *Life* (August 26, 1946), pp. 92-105. Communal life in agricultural village between Tientsin and Peiping, where "the horizon of understanding coincides with the visual horizon."

"A Reporter at Large: The Communization of Crow Village," *The New Yorker* (July 27, 1946), pp. 38-47. Important article for determining Hersey's political awareness. Some generalizations on Chinese Communism superimposed on objective account of village life. "Impressive progress" noted by comparison with inertia of Central Government.

"A Reporter at Large: Hiroshima," *The New Yorker* (August 31, 1946), pp. 15-68. Original publication. Reprinted in *Here to Stay*.

"A Reporter at Large: The Ingathering of Exiles," *The New Yorker* (November 24, 1951), pp. 92-113. Sensitive observations on immigration problems of Israel: "a generation that represents the most wonderfully resolved internationalism on earth today, but . . . also a generation into which a burning and bitter nationalism is being bred."

"A Reporter at Large: Journey Toward a Sense of Being Treated Well," *The New Yorker* (March 2, 1957), pp. 39-87. Odyssey of the Fekete family from Budapest to an Austrian relocation center. Reprinted in *Here To Stay*.

"A Reporter at Large: Long Haul with Variables," *The New Yorker* (September 8, 1945), pp. 44-57. How the return of the 86th Division reflected the difficulties of bringing 4,100,000 American soldiers home from Europe and the Pacific.

"A Reporter at Large: Over the Mad River," *The New Yorker* (September 17, 1955), pp. 118-40. The rescue of an old woman from a flood-menaced tenement in Winsted, Connecticut, following Hurricane Diane. Reprinted in *Here To Stay*.

"A Reporter in China," *The New Yorker* (May 18, 1946), pp. 59-69; May 25, 1946, pp. 54-69. Misunderstandings incurred in transporting Chinese Nationalist troops on American LST's.

"A Reporter in Shanghai," *The New Yorker* (March 23, 1946), pp. 32-36. Problems of a Western businessman trying to resume operations.

"Ricksha No. 34," *Life* (June 3, 1946), pp. 63-70. The leading ricksha puller in Peiping serves as an example of China's strengths and weaknesses.

"Russia Likes Plays Too," *Time* (October 23, 1944), pp. 48-50. Prospects of Moscow's theater compared favorably with New York's.

"A Short Wait," *The New Yorker* (June 14, 1947), pp. 27-29. Short story of the cold reception a European Jewish refugee receives at the hands of her wealthy American relatives.

"A Short Talk with Erlanger," *Life* (October 29, 1945), pp. 108-22. The army's use of narco-synthesis in treating psychiatric cases. Reprinted in *Here To Stay*.

"Survival," *The New Yorker* (June 17, 1944), pp. 31-34. Account of Lieutenant John F. Kennedy's exploit after the destruction of PT-109. Reprinted in *Here To Stay*.

"Three Airmen," *Life* (May 29, 1944), pp. 67-73. Brief text accompanying portraits of generals James Doolittle, Bernt Balchen, and Claire Chennault.

"USS Borie's Last Battle," *Life* (December 13, 1943), pp. 104-116. Destroyer action in the North Atlantic.

"USS LCI 226," *Life* (March 27, 1944), pp. 53-61. Possibly the most euphoric of Hersey's wartime dispatches. "His men had come through many trials, and he was glad he was their captain."

"The Wayward Press: Conference in Room 474," *The New Yorker* (December 16, 1950), pp. 78-90. On official handling of the news during the Korean War.

"Why Do Students Bog Down on First R?" *Life* (May 24, 1954), pp. 136-50. Based on investigations of Fairfield (Conn.) group appointed by the Citizen's School Study Council.

"Why Were You Sent Out Here?" *The Atlantic Monthly*, CLXXIX (February, 1947), 88-91. Short story. An older marine officer is repelled by a younger officer's acts, only to realize that the man is an image of himself at an earlier age. Peiping, 1946.

"Yale '36—Look at Them Now," *Harper's Magazine*, CCV (September 1952), 21-28. Brief survey and briefer reminiscence.

3. Plays based on novels

LAMPELL, MILLARD, *The Wall*. Opened at the Billy Rose Theatre, New York, December, 1960. ("Honest, but curiously unmoving," *Theatre Arts Monthly* [December, 1960]. See also Millard Lampell, "Bringing 'The Wall' to the Stage," *Mid-stream*, VI [Autumn, 1960], 14-19, and George M. Ross, "*The Wall* on Broadway," *Commentary*, XXXI [January, 1961], 66-69.)

OSBORN, PAUL, *A Bell for Adano*. Opened at the Cort Theatre, New York, December, 1944. (". . . the tone and the intent are not grave and passionate; they are only amiably and pleasantly significant. This understood, the whole thing settles down into a very pleasant evening, well performed and gently conveyed." Stark Young in *The New Republic* [December 25, 1944] p. 867.) *A Bell for Adano* was also made into a motion picture by Twentieth Century Fox (1945) and a ninety-minute television musical (June 3, 1956).

SHYRE, PAUL, *The Child Buyer*. Presented by the University of Michigan Professional Theatre Program, Ann Arbor, Michigan. (See Tom Prideaux, "The Child Buyer," *Life* [April 3, 1964], p. 14. Favorable review, stating that Hersey and Shyre offered the play to the Michigan group in preference to a Broadway production. The play was given a trial performance by the Theatre Arts Department of the University of California, Los Angeles, in 1963.)

SECONDARY SOURCES

Very little has been written about Hersey and his work. The items selected below form a small cross-section of book reviews to go along with the few periodical references that could be termed "articles." Fiedler and Simon are listed for the sake of illustrating the offhand observations which assail the writer.

BURTON, ARTHUR. "Existential Conceptions in John Hersey's Novel, *The Child Buyer*," *Journal of Existential Psychology*, II (Fall, 1961), 243-58.

COUSINS, NORMAN. "John Hersey," *Saturday Review of Literature* (March 4, 1950), p. 15. A reprint of Cousins' article in the March, 1950, *Book-of-the-Month-Club News*. Comment on the novel is incidental to praise of the man, who has "a conviction that human values, human failings, and human experiences are the basic building blocks of writing."

DAICHES, DAVID, "Record and Statement," *Commentary* (April, 1950), p. 385-88. A review of *The Wall* ("a splendid and moving treatment of one man's understanding and humanity"), which comments on Hersey's record of "his own noble and almost desperate sympathy" and sees Noach Levinson as a projection of Hersey himself.

ESPEY, JOHN J. *Minor Heresies.* New York: Alfred A. Knopf, Inc., 1945.

——. *The Other City.* New York: Alfred A. Knopf, Inc., 1950.

——. *Tales Out of School.* New York, Alfred A. Knopf, Inc., 1947. Sketches of the childhood and youth of an American son of missionaries stationed in Shanghai. Espey is Hersey's contemporary, the author of a novel (*Anniversaries*, 1964) and a study of Ezra Pound's *Hugh Selwyn Mauberley.*

FIEDLER, LESLIE A. "The Novel in the Post-Political World," *Partisan Review* (Summer, 1956), pp. 358-65. *A Single Pebble* and Nelson Algren's *A Walk on the Wild Side* led Fiedler to despairing comment on the contemporary American novel in this famous diatribe. ("To read a group of novels nowadays is a depressing experience.") The review is attacked several times by novelists contributing to Granville Hicks's symposium, *The Living Novel* (1957). Fiedler denies that Hersey is a novelist and states that "he writes fiction (or pretends to) only as a strategy for getting his point of view across." The real animus may lie in such a statement as: "I must confess in all frankness that I find Hersey's sentiments so piously unexceptionable as to be intolerable."

GEISMAR, MAXWELL. "John Hersey: The Revival of Conscience," *American Moderns.* New York: Hill and Wang, 1958, pp. 180-86. (Includes Geismar's review of *The Wall* in *Saturday Review of Literature* [March 4, 1950], pp. 14, 16.) The most balanced of the favorable comments on Hersey. Geismar praises him as a social novelist in a period when "social themes" are suspect. The critic is shrewd at the expense of cleverness in the following: "One may suspect that there is a whole psychic area roped off from Hersey's consciousness, and that he sees people in terms of a situation—or a crisis—rather than in and for themselves."

GUILFOIL, KELSEY. "John Hersey: Fact and Fiction," *English Journal,* XXXIX (September, 1950), 355-60. Routine consideration of whether Hersey is a journalist or a novelist. After his first four books, it was too soon to tell.

MCDONNELL, T. P. "Hersey's Allegorical Novels," *Catholic World,* XCV, (July, 1962), 240-45.

SIMON, JOHN. "Theatre Chronicle," *Hudson Review,* XIII (Winter, 1961), 591. Lacking Fiedler's wit, a vicious observation on Hersey is Simon's passing notice of the Broadway production of *The*

Wall. "Writers who are artistically ill-equipped, i.e., morally unqualified, to deal with these situations are merely lice in the hair of such disasters. . . ."

"Talk of the Town," *Newsweek* (September 9, 1946), pp. 69-71. Account of how *Hiroshima* was written.

TRILLING, DIANA. "Fiction in Review," *The Nation* (February 12, 1944), pp. 194-95. A review of *A Bell for Adano*.

Index

DATE DUE

GAYLORD